The Trouble with the Church
A Call for Renewal

A Call for Renewal .

Translated and Edited by
JOHN W. DOBERSTEIN

THE TROUBLE
WITH THE CHURCH

HELMUT THIELICKE

HARPER & ROW, PUBLISHERS
New York

C-Q

Contents

Translator's Note : vii

Preface : xv

THE PLIGHT OF PREACHING : 1

OUR CREDIBILITY : 3

THE DICHOTOMY OF CHRISTIAN EXISTENCE : 11

THE PATHOLOGY OF SPIRITUAL EXISTENCE : 14

THE INTELLECTUAL DEMAND OF PREACHING : 19

THE PREACHER AS A HELPLESS SOLOIST : 25

THE DUALISM BETWEEN PREACHER AND
    PROFESSOR : 28

THE DICTATORSHIP OF THE LISTENERS : 31

THE DECAY OF THE LANGUAGE OF PREACHING : 33

MODERNITY—VENEER OR SUBSTANCE? : 38

THE BREAKDOWN OF WORDS AND THEIR REVIVAL : 42

CLERICAL PROMOTERS : 48

THE LANGUAGE OF THE PROFESSIONALS : 50

THE FEAR OF SAYING TOO LITTLE : 52

TWO THEOLOGIANS IN DIALOGUE : 56

A BRIEF LOOK IN THE SERMON LABORATORY : 61

ABSTRACT MAN—THE WRONG MAN TO ADDRESS : 65

THE MAN WHO DOES NOT EXIST : 70

THE TRIUMPH OF DISENGAGEMENT AND BOREDOM : 77

THE FLIGHT IN BUSYWORK AND LITURGICAL ARTCRAFT : 81

THE DOMINION OF THE PURISTS AND ANTIQUARIANS : 85

THE PERVERSION OF THE PROTESTANT PRINCIPLE : 89

THE PSEUDO-SACRED : 94

THE LITURGY AND THE SERMON : 97

COMPLETE THE REFORMATION OR
    RECATHOLICIZATION? : 102

THE MISERY AND THE OPPORTUNITY OF THE NATIONAL
    CHURCH : 110

THE SEARCH FOR THE *"Sitz im Leben"* : 112

A NEW STYLE OF PROCLAMATION: PARENTS
    GROUPS : 118

CONFIRMATION—THE THORNY QUESTION : 120

SUFFERING LOVE FOR THE CHURCH : 126

IN CONCLUSION : 129

Notes : 131

Sources of the Epigraphs : 133

Index : 135

Translator's Note

This is a book that is critical of the church, but written with the passion of one who unequivocally takes his stand within the church. Professor Thielicke, writing to me about it, expressed some concern about its relevance for others, since it is addressed to the continental situation. "In large parts of it typically German conditions are characterized, but you can judge of this. It would seem to me necessary that this time you should not merely translate the book, but also revise it on your own, i.e., leave out parts and possibly rewrite others for the American situation. Would it not be nice if in this way we wrote a book together and also indicated this on the title page?"

Despite these generous words, however, I have chosen not to make any alterations in the text except those which "normal" translation would permit. Indeed, I think the reader will again and again be struck by the fact that these basic problems of the church are identical, no matter whether we confront them in Germany or in America. Nevertheless Professor Thielicke's kindness makes me bold to speak at greater length than might be called for in a translator's note, since in an extensive correspondence with him over the years the "trouble with the church" and especially its preaching has been a recurring theme of common concern.

We are being told that the day of preaching is over and that it is a vain hope ever to revive it. "Today the pulpit is not what it used to be. The preacher simply is not heard. It is poor strategy to depend on the pulpit." No one will quarrel with the facts about the state of preaching today; but we may well challenge the conclusion that is drawn. It is a commonplace to say that we have gone through a generation in which the minister has allowed himself to become at best a "pastoral director" and consequently preaching has degenerated. Then, having produced this kind of preaching, which, in all honesty, is not worth listening to, which, as Luther said, would not entice a dog from behind a warm stove, which, indeed, people will not sit through, and having fished with this "melancholy bait," we say that preaching is no longer effective. Of course it isn't effective; how could it be? It all smacks of the argument of the liturgical enthusiast, who proves beyond a shadow of a doubt by his own flaccid vaporings that preaching is no good, and then proceeds to say, "See, what people want from me and the church is the liturgy—more sacraments and more frequent celebration." Ministers who hold this opinion about preaching should be forbidden to preach; it is an unconscionable presumption for them to require me or any laymen to sit quietly, enduring what is only a trial of the flesh and the spirit, and listen to what this "slovenly" (Thielicke's word) defeatist hands out as his weekly chore. Before God and in all loyalty and love for the church, I have a right to say this. What I and many of my colleagues hear, however, is that people want good preaching. Again and again highly intelligent lay people, who love the church and the Lord of the church, say to us: Why can't we have better preaching? We do not hear them asking for more liturgy, more form, more organization, more discussion groups, more this, more that. In the introduction to the first volume of Thielicke's sermons, I referred to Paul Althaus's statement that people today are not tired of preaching, but tired of our preaching. This, I believe, is true. Wherever we find, even in this day, a vital, living congregation we find at its center vital preaching. The man who cannot preach and will not devote himself to it with the best that is in him is not likely to be any more effective, credible, and convincing, so far as the gospel is concerned, in a discussion group, a cell group, a buzz group (what a horrible conception!), as a conductor of ceremonies, or as an organizer and manipulator of God's human beings. All this is not to say, of course, that we think it is possible to revive nineteenth-century patterns or that other forms of ministry need not be sought. But to tell us, as we are being told *ad nauseam* in articles, addresses, and books, all with the air of the great theological diagnostician, that we must seek ever new forms of ministry is to utter a platitude (the church's pastoral ministry, when it has been true to its commission, has always been committed to seek men wherever they are and in whatever way they must be approached in order that they may hear). But to downgrade the pulpit will be fatal.

Another factor, in theological education especially, has contributed to the discouragement of preaching: the preoccupation with the problems of exegesis. We allow ourselves to be confused to the point where we and our students no longer know what or how to preach. We avidly read the effusions of those who have read a little of Bonhoeffer and Bultmann and let it go to their heads. The fact is that Bonhoeffer would squirm to read what these theologians, and even bishops, have extrapolated from a few tentative and private ruminations in his prison cell.

(Incidentally, this reminds me of another development that has recently depressed me. We are aware that something has happened to Lent and there are always clever fellows who have a solution, one being to reduce its length. Now evangelical Protestants have never had any interest in Lent as a period of fasting. The only way to give it content has been to regard it as the Passion season with central emphasis on the proclamation of the cross: otherwise we could have no concern to preserve it as a tradition. Indeed, many Lenten sermons I have heard in my lifetime have had to indulge in great preliminary puffings and blowings to make it clear that Lent is not a season of fasting in the medieval sense. Strange that the church did exactly what its Epistle and Gospel for Ash

Wednesday tells us not to do! So we have no interest in preserving Lent *per se*. But when on a Wednesday evening in Lent we are asked to attend a discussion of the bishop's highly successful and highly questionable book instead of hearing the proclamation of the cross—well, as far as I am concerned, I am willing to say: Good-by Lent and perhaps good riddance!—even though I believe that this would be only another evidence of the church's loss of nerve and loss of central substance in its preaching.)

To resume our reference to the current overemphasis upon hermeneutics, Thielicke in a letter speaks of it as a movement which "has led us into complete sterility." Europeans are tired of it, but Americans seem not to notice and go "marching cheerfully into a blind alley. When we deal with the subject of preaching, why do we inquire precisely of those who not only do not preach themselves but also have alarmingly jammed the guns of the younger generation? Not long ago I visited a colleague in the hospital. He said: 'What's wrong with the young theologians? They no longer dare to make a single statement of their own. Here they read to us the sermons of E——, which nobody can understand. Nor does anybody want to hear this preaching any more.'

"When we study sermons—and how good and necessary this is!—we ought, in my opinion, to take a number of model sermons from various proveniences, perhaps even from various countries and confessions, and determine whether they really are sermons as we consider they should be. In so far as they are sermons—and this seems to me to be very important—one should determine on the basis of these actual examples: What is the exegesis behind them? How do they move from the text to the sermon? How is man in his real situation seen in these sermons? To what extent therefore are they really addressed to the man of today? In this way one could analyze the preaching situation and learn to preach.

"Instead of doing this we go seeking advice from people who cannot preach themselves and, what is more, deprive others of all ability to preach. I have no doubt whatsoever of the subjective honesty of their intentions and their willingness not to make preaching too easy. Nevertheless, what is behind it is a completely sterile theology. The whole misery can be summed up in one sentence: Preachers no longer understand texts, they rather seek to understand understanding."

This little book reminds me of one by another great preacher—*Heralds of God*, written some twenty years ago by James S. Stewart (New York: Charles Scribner's Sons, 1946), and especially these words: "Do not listen to the foolish talk which suggests that, for this twentieth century, the preaching of the Word is an anachronism, and that the pulpit, having served its purpose, must now be displaced by press or radio, discussion group or Brains Trust, and finally vanish from the scene. As long as God sets his image on the soul, and men are restless till they rest in him, so long will the preacher's task persist, and his voice be heard through all the clamor of the world."

Thielicke's courageous address to his fellow Christians and fellow ministers on the church's escape into liturgism, its flight into busyness, and its increasing dependence on centralization and bureaucratic procedures provides us all with the kind of shaking up that we need. I, for one, am grateful for it.

JOHN W. DOBERSTEIN

Mount Airy, Philadelphia
March, 1965

It is as if a new Adam must come in order to give new names to everything.—*Margarete Susman, philosopher*

If you (reverend sirs) are not able to find the way back to an unconditional self-criticism . . . which will make possible a new beginning, no advertising techniques in the world will be able to stop the end from coming.

If God has forsaken you, what advice can we poor advertising men give you? Men will not stop seeking God, but they will choose other mediators. Do you no longer understand, reverend sirs, what it was that actually gave that little group of apostles on the day of Pentecost such tremendous power that it was sufficient to transform the face of the Western world? These were not advertising media in the ordinary sense . . . , it was rather the influencing power of faith, an unshakable faith in the mission of Christ and the redemption in life and death which accomplished the miracle. Because you yourselves no longer feel the influencing power of faith within you, you try to substitute tactical cleverness for the missing suggestive aid of a strong soul. And when you do that you sink ever deeper into the realm of no response.
        —*Hans Domizlaff, advertising man*

Nevertheless it cannot be said that the altars are deserted or that prayers are no longer offered up. . . . Bloy's statement *"Dieu se retire"* is therefore closer to the facts of the situation. . . . Where there was faith, a need remains; it keeps groping with a thousand arms for a new object. This is the restlessness which is generated by the disappearance [of faith]. . . . This is the time of seeking, of great wanderings and departures, of true and false prophets, of lonely night watches.
        —*Ernst Jünger, writer*

If anybody thinks we can simply begin our confessional Christianity where orthodoxy stopped as a mere relic of the past, he is being . . . unhistorical; for a fondness for things antiquarian is not a sense of history, but simply a hobby.

Can Christianity be of God if it exists only for a number of "quiet in the land"?—*Martin Kähler, theologian*

Faith is not a thing which one "loses," we merely cease to shape our lives by it.—*Georges Bernanos, writer*

Preface

—He who takes a position exposes himself.

For many people what is written here may be an offense. But, believe me, it was a pressing need that compelled me to speak. I could not bear any longer *not* to say what is said in the following pages. In the concluding part of the book I state what my motives were.

The following reflections fall into two groups, some sections intended for ministers of the church and others which are meant for the despisers of the church. Even what I have to say in the way of internal criticism (*intra muros*, as it were), in the way of concern and counsel with respect to the failure of our preaching is also intended for the ears of those outside the church, that they may get some idea of what we are grappling with. I have observed that people who have disassociated themselves from everything that happens in the church do not like to be addressed in special tracts which are all too clearly beamed at them. In so far as they are still possessed of that fruitful curiosity which dismisses nothing and is open to everything, they prefer to be the "little mouse" who simply listens to what the gentlemen are saying. This, I hope, will happen here.

What follows is only a fragment of what I would really like to say. And what I regard as most important has not gone unnoticed. If Protestantism were to hold a council like that of the Vatican in Rome today, I would present to the council fathers who were out for reform some of the following for consideration (and at the same time indicate to them that there was still a large stock of material waiting to be dealt with at a second session). I believe I have a pretty fair idea of the answer I would get from the "conservative" council fathers, whom we have in our circles too. They would say: "Give us less diagnosis and write more prescriptions." For it is rather remarkable that in the church the "conservatives" do often have the disastrous inclination to apply their energy less to the searching penetration of what is given than to take the given doctrine, the given institution, the given Christian common sense and make it manipulable and then transmit it to men. (However, it will not be easy for the reader to classify the author's opinions as "conservative" or "modern.") Often it is precisely in the so-called conservative camp that you will find the cleverest and most efficient "managers." No wonder that they would rather have prescriptions than diagnoses! I suspect, however, that we must first get a relentlessly clear picture of ourselves before we can find new ways and break out of the blind alleys we are in. The very way in which we exercise this self-criticism and the unsparing way in which we devote ourselves to it will in itself show whether we are taking the gospel seriously. For the point of the gospel is that God will not drop us no matter what or who we are. But anybody who has a merciful judge loses the inhibition to be hard in his judgment of himself. He is freed to be objective. And objectivity too lies within the horizon of redemption. But empty hands are given the promise that they will be filled. Only he who anxiously tries to hold on to the given will find that he has been betrayed and sold out.

This is a personal word and a personal concern and distress, and I dispense with caution and any attempt to guard and qualify my statements at every point. This requires a different style from that which is found in my academic works and sermon volumes. Though I have endeavored to be graphic and to illustrate as much as possible, I am under no illusion that occasionally severe demands will not be made upon the reader and that he will not be challenged to do some thinking.

Deus bene vertat.

The Trouble with the Church
A Call for Renewal

The Plight of Preaching

Anybody who keeps in mind the goals which the Reformation once set for itself can only be appalled at what has happened in the church of Luther and Calvin to the very thing which its fathers regarded as the source and spring of Christian faith and life, namely, preaching. In the hectic bustle of ecclesiastical routine it appears to be relegated more and more to the margin of things. The big city pastor must spend his evenings sitting in meetings of esoteric church organizations where he is always seeing the same faces. During the day he is being chewed up by instructional classes, occasional services, pastoral calls, and the Moloch of his bureaucracy. All this pulverizes him in the mortar of that tiny sector of a pluralistic society which is called the "church"—a sector which the dwellers in the gigantic secularized provinces of life hardly notice. The pastor has the feeling that he is performing this ministry almost to the exclusion of any public notice whatso-ever. And as he drives and runs about, carrying with him the commission to proclaim a message that would revolutionize life, he may be oppressed on the one hand by the thought of the tremendous contradiction between the claim and the promise of this message and on the other by the utter immovability of the deeply rutted tracks in which he must move. What is happening? And where is there even the slightest indication that a light is shining in the world and that the salt is at work in the soil, keeping it from going sour? Because a man so harassed is threatened by

1

the onset of melancholia, he may also be oppressed by the institutional unreality and unveracity in the midst of which he does his work: the public and legally privileged consolidation of this ecclesiastical establishment which has no equivalent inner authority. The self-critical question which he asks himself might be this: What would the institutional framework in which I perform my ministry look like if it were not put at the disposal of the great mass of people who pay church taxes and possess baptismal certificates and yet do not participate in the life of the church, but rather represented whatever real living faith is actually in it? Preparing a sermon requires some verve and inspiration, but here there seems to be nothing but a leaden weight holding a man down. It requires concentration and composure, but here there is nothing but a busyness that distracts and dissipates a man's mind.

But it is not only the *place* where the preaching is done that has been so dubiously relegated to the periphery of life and thus in an organic sense displaced. Actually preaching itself has decayed and disintegrated to the point where it is close to the stage of dying. As a student I once attended a service in the local congregation with a noted teacher of theology. I have not forgotten (but actually remember almost word for word) what this professor said to me after listening to the utterly miserable sermon. "The first thing I do when I enter the church," he said, "is to look around and note with sadness that hardly one of my colleagues from the other faculties is sitting in the pews. But when the sermon is over, I usually say to myself: What a good thing that none of them was there!" He went on to say, "I do not demand that this harassed man in the pulpit give me a rhetorical treat or brilliant food for my interest. I do not even expect a thorough exegesis, for perhaps he could not get down to preparing his sermon until Saturday evening. But one thing I could well do without and that is the peculiar tone, the same old tune." He was referring to the usual criticism: the mere grinding out of a routine vocabulary—God, grace, sin, justification—which produces a kind of Christian gobbledegook that never gets under anybody's skin and at most elicits the reaction: Well, that's the way the minister *has* to speak, but what's it to me? "A man's own peculiar tone is everything; he who does not hold on to it gives up an inner freedom which is the only thing that can make real speech possible." It was Hugo von Hofmannsthal who said this long ago.[1]

If I am not mistaken, the man of our generation has a very sensitive instinct for routine phrases. Advertising and propaganda has thoroughly accustomed him to this. He knows that the adman's commendations of a brand-name product (or of a political system!) do not express the personal conviction of the man who is speaking, but that they are stereotyped mechanical phrases which are intended to wear a hole in a stubbornly stony psyche by means of a constant drip. Anybody who wants to know whether a particular soft drink is really as good as the advertising man on the television screen says it is cannot simply believe the phonetically amplified recommendations, but must find out whether this man actually drinks this soft drink at home when he is not in public. Does the preacher himself drink what he hands out in the pulpit? This is the question that is being asked by the child of our time who has been burned by publicity and advertising.

Our Credibility

The man of our time would certainly be doing an injustice to the pastor if he supposed that he might possibly be a hypocrite. I know a great number of ministers, but I do not know a single one who secretly swears by a "different brand of soft drink" from the one he is advocating. And yet, however unjust this question may be on the surface (it certainly is not a question of gross hypocrisy), it may nevertheless point to some rather depressing and doubtful questions in the background. Then the thrust of the question must be: What does it mean to be convinced of something and to advocate it as the "truth"?

Obviously, anything that has the dignity of a conviction requires something more than regarding it to be true. Merely regarding something as true—this can be nothing more than a nonbinding, noncommittal opinion. And we know very well—say, from the opinion polls—how mere opinions come into being, that often they are merely the functions of a particular milieu, that they are subject to tradition's law of inertia and pressures of what "people are saying," and that besides they can be manipulated and "created." Who, then, can prove to us that Christian opinion has not been created in the same way? Is there not much that supports this? Could anybody today who comes out of the Christian tradition really feel that the truth which is here being advocated is discovery that is relevant to his life? Is it not far too remote from the things that normally interest and move him: the evening television program, his concern with the relative social prestige he has with his neighbor, the next football game, the anticipation of a vacation? Can anybody explain this repeated threshing out of the same old grain, which has long since become empty chaff except by concluding that at some time the man's family pressed the threshing flail into his hand and now the conditioned reflexes ground into him by the Christian tradition keep him threshing away even though there has long since been nothing left that could generate any living fruit? Could not *this* be the so-called Christian opinion which is expounded in the pulpits? And could not these conditioned reflexes of the Christian tradition be quite compatible with subjective honesty? After all, even the negative psychiatrists of the ideological systems, who use this Pavlovian doctrine of reflexes to manipulate the human psyche, seek to produce stereotyped convictions which their victims then actually and honestly believe they possess. Are they not then literally filled with self-accusation and their new faith—say, in Mao Tse-tung? The only question is whether we can accept anything they say.

The criticism behind such skeptical questions can be summed

up as follows. It is not sufficient for us that the preacher is subjectively imbued with the correctness of his conviction and that he is therefore not a conscious hypocrite. (We certainly do not think he is that disreputable.) In order to be able to form a judgment concerning his credibility (and here again we come back to the soft drink illustration) we would have to know whether he lives, whether he really "exists," in the house of the dogmas he proclaims.

This means that what the preacher says in the pulpit must have a relationship to what fills the rest of his existence. Sure, he is a nice, pleasant, affable fellow. But I ask you, when does anything about Christ come out in his ordinary human conversation? When is this name uttered quite naturally when he is talking to me about the weather or about my son? He is a man of culture. Whenever there is a problem play in the movies or in the theater he is sure to be there, and not long ago I saw him at an exhibition of Emil Nolde's paintings. When he talks about these things his voice has that natural and casual tone, which indicates that what is said has become a natural and obvious part of the intellectual organism. But when he talks about "sacred" things, the very timbre of his voice (though it has not a trace of "pulpit tone") shows that he is talking about something which has been brought in from some faraway region, something that now lies like a foreign body, like a meteor from another planet in the normal landscape of his life. When he talks about Kafka or Tennessee Williams he is "all there." But the other thing he seems to have to "drag in." Nor do they ever occur together; it is almost as if there were two spheres, two compartments in him which are not connected by a door and therefore have no vital communication with each other.

So we ask, does he really live in his doctrinal house? Does he bring Kafka and Bert Brecht and Tennessee Williams into that house? Does he take his enjoyment of a good joke into that house? In other words, does he live in it? Does he do his *thinking*, feeling, and willing in it? Or are the pulpit and his study places outside of this world, separated from the pleasant normalities of his existence?

The fact that he works hard on his preaching—that he studies the Bible, and ponders theological problems—this would still be no proof that he drinks his own "soft drink." All this could be, as we said, only a conditioned reflex, an effect of the categorical imperative which demands that he be faithful in his job. The question is rather whether he quenches his own thirst with the Bible, just as he satisfied the thirst of his intellectual and human interests in the theater or in association with his friends. If I see a breach, if I see no connection, between his Christian and his human existence—so argues the average person consciously or unconsciously—then I am inclined to accept the conclusion that he himself is not living in the house of his own preaching, but has settled down somewhere beside it, and that therefore the center of gravity in his life lies elsewhere.

This reminds me of an experience we had after the last war. It was an experience that was confirmed again and again at numerous conferences with prominent men of the church. We met many pastors who had returned from long military service or long and grievous imprisonment. Both of these experiences had confronted them with the boundary situations of human life and subjected them to an exceedingly elemental fate. They had been forcibly ejected from the ecclesiastical ghetto and exposed to the directest kind of human contacts. Everybody thought that this would have a very discernible effect upon the way they preached. If before they had perhaps been rather colorless and withdrawn from life, now surely they would be vital and saturated with the juices of suffering and real life. That hope increased as one listened to them recounting their experiences; everything they said was taut and compact, there was no false tone, and therefore we were stirred. But once they were in the pulpit, all this immediacy disappeared. The same old dull monotonous waters flowed down the same old accustomed channel. Even that which still retained the tone of immediacy, the man's own personal tone, had again become general and colorless. And whereas we used to be inclined to think that "the whole man had been recast and transformed in the fires of war," in the pulpit he appeared to go on without any perceptible break from where he left off in 1939.

There was something rather appalling about this and one asked oneself how one could explain the fact that a man's preaching could remain so completely untouched by his experiences. To be sure, there were exceptions, and we were happy to note the evidences of spiritual growth. In these cases the terrible experiences had been spiritually assimilated and theologically mastered, and they then led to a form of preaching that—to compare something small with something great—reminded one of the prophets. For the message of the prophets was directly interfused with the time and the history in which they lived. There the historical figures (Cyrus and Nebuchadnezzar), the great floods and the wonderful deliverances, the public and private sins, were set down "in the light of God's face" and made transparent so that the judgment and grace of God could be seen through them.

In most cases where this spiritual growth took place and one could see that the preaching of the message had been vivified it was because these men had gone through these terrible experiences in a peculiar way. That is to say, the preacher had had to go on preaching during this time in his life, in the cauldron of Stalingrad or in the midst of the terrors of the bombings. In this way he was compelled every day afresh to break through his own fears, terrors, and troubles and look to the hills from whence comes our help. He had to learn in his own person to cope with the apocalyptic situation which threw the average person into shock, panic, or numbness and see it *sub specie aeternitatis*—simply because he had to climb up a pulpit or some makeshift platform to tell his beaten and beleaguered listeners that all this had something to do with God, with his judgment and visitation.

Thus life and preaching came into the closest possible contact. For in *this* situation it was virtually impossible to talk about sin and grace in a merely general sense. What was merely general and unrelated to the situation would simply stick in a man's throat. I should either have to keep my mouth shut or say something for this particular hour. But in order to be able to speak to this moment, it would have to become for me something more than a particle in the stream of time which I was passively allowing to carry me along. I would have to relate this portion of time to eternity and digest it spiritually.

In this way I would be subjected to the discipline of concrete preaching and I would be set down in the stern, inexorable school of the Holy Spirit. I would be compelled vicariously, as it were, to stand off from the terror of that hour for the sake of those who would hear my message along with me, though in time I was right in the midst of it; whereas usually it is said that only after an interval of time does one arrive at a balanced and mature judgment. But here one had to preach "in this moment." And therefore the distance from the immediate situation that had to be gained was not a distance of time at all. It was rather that the dimension of eternity came to my aid. *Because* I did not merely live through and suffer this hour and its meaninglessness in a creaturely way, but rather asked the question whether God was not thinking his higher thoughts about its meaninglessness, whether and in what way even it was a chapter in the story of salvation and therefore was not excluded from God's great compendium of history—*because* I was forced to put this question (it was tremendously urgent, for immediately I had to mount the pulpit, immediately the people would be intently waiting to see whether my words would miss the point or whether my message would still be heard above the hoofbeats of the apocalyptic horseman)—*because* I was compelled to ask this question, the distance, the perspective, the dimension of eternity was granted. That could only be a miracle of the Spirit. Only he who was thus

lifted above the hour was able to speak to it; then he was close to
that hour in a completely new and undreamed-of way.

But what about those who went through far more terrible experiences and now after the war simply go on preaching in the same
old conventional and falsely detached way? Do we solve this
vexing puzzle perhaps by saying that they experienced that phase
of history in a "creaturely," not a "spiritual," way (which is by no
means to say that this may not have been done in a very
brave and humanly impressive way)? Or that perhaps they were
too exhausted, too hungry, too desperate, too louse-ridden to be
able to make the effort to meditate, or even to read the Bible and
gain this spiritual perspective, this distance from the hour?

Anybody who is inclined to answer these questions in the
affirmative can make this diagnosis only in a spirit which is devoid
of any Pharisaism. He can do so only in gratitude for the hard
grace of God which had compelled him perhaps by reason of his
calling (and not because of his particular theological qualifications) to break away—often by desperate and hopeless effort—
from despair and hopelessness, to detach himself from it and let
the Psalms, the Prophets, and the Gospels have greater power
over him than the frightful hour which was in fact threatening to
overwhelm him.

But as for the preachers whose message is not infused with what
they have gone through, it would in fact appear to be true that the
center of gravity in their lives may lie somewhere else than in their
message, that possibly their house of doctrine lies somewhere
alongside of this life which they experience with such great inten-
sity.

This is the point, it seems to me, where the secret distrust of
Christian preaching is smoldering. Behind all the obvious and
superficial criticisms—such as that the sermon is boring, remote
from life, irrelevant—there is, I am convinced, this ultimate reservation, namely, that the man who bores others must also be boring
himself. And the man who bores himself is not really living in

what he—so boringly—hands out. "Where your treasure is, there will your heart be also"—in this case the treasure of the heart seems not to be identical with what it is commending to others. The attractions by which this heart is moved seem to come from some other source. So we miss the very thing that my teacher of theology was talking about: the peculiar, personal tone. For that peculiar tone will be immediately audible if the speaker himself is in what he says, if he gives of himself and puts his whole heart into it.

Naturally, the preacher himself knows this, even if he is one of these unfortunates who live "alongside" of their message. Then sometimes—and again not hypocritically but in the honest belief that it is as it should be—the vox humana is blended with the trick rhetorical note and he steps on the swell to produce the ring of conviction. For he knows theologically that the gospel demands the whole man. So the full phonetic effect must be produced and the genuine note of the heart must be sounded.

Even though this may not be rank hypocrisy it is nevertheless ultimately dishonest. For even Jesus did not think of hypocrisy as conscious shamming; he never caricatured the Pharisees in this way! What he meant by hypocrisy was an objective contradiction in one's own existence, a contradiction which the person involved may not be aware of at all. This antinomy may be present, for example, when a person reverently participates in the liturgy of worship but at the same time sabotages the commandment of God by being heartless with his neighbor (Matt. 5:23). So the contradiction consists in the fact that on the one hand we are on the side of redemption, but that on the other hand these are unredeemed areas within us which are still untouched by the renewing breath of the Spirit.

Perhaps we may put it this way. The heart may be beating for God, it may also be really gripped by his grace, and it may be a very devout heart; but it has not yet pumped the blood to the extremities of the body. There are still some numb parts which have not yet been reached by this revived circulation of the blood. I may not yet be aware, for example, that my sex life or my business life *also* have something to do with God (that therefore God by no means confines himself to some religious province within me and leaves me free to manage the other sectors of myself or just lets them go on functioning in their own autonomy).

The Dichotomy of Christian Existence

I once encountered a vivid example of this. A very well-to-do church councilman had invited me to tea in his very fine and tastefully furnished home. I expressed my regret that during the war even this gem of a house had not been spared by the bombs, leaving only a small portion of it standing (though this had now been beautifully restored). His reply was, "Don't talk about regret. Even in this loss I experienced the grace of God." And the first thing I thought was: How devout this man is, how humble he is—and what a superficial and sentimental way to have addressed him! Then he went on to say: "God left me with just enough room so that I did not have to take in any refugees after the war." I shall not now expatiate upon the shock which this alternating hot and cold shower of statements produced in me. I confine myself simply to making this theological point: The man was really devout, he worshiped and prayed, and he was really concerned with the social and ethical aspects of his business. But obviously it had never occurred to him that the housing shortage had anything to do with one's relationship to God and our neighbor. He had failed to see that this problem, like every other area of life, is related to the message which he had accepted and affirmed in his heart. His spiritual house stood apart, separated from and unconnected with the rest of his life. The words "housing shortage" and "personal comfort" seemed not to have any relevance so far as his faith was concerned; they appeared to evoke other passions that had nothing to do with God. The devout heart had not yet pumped the blood down to these members; the extremities remained numb.

Perhaps this anecdote is typical of the situation of Protestantism in general. Luther brought a message for this "heart." He showed that the heart no longer needed to burden itself with scruples about its own wickedness, but that God wanted to have mercy, that he wanted to be near to it, even though it is filled to the brim with evil thoughts, motives, and urges. The theological thinking of the Protestant churches has been largely confined to this message of the new status of the heart before God. But it has not considered (or too little considered) that the heart controls an entire circulatory system and that it must also supply blood to the extremities. But hasn't it taken an awfully long time (in Germany at any rate until National Socialism came and rabidly claimed total dominion over all the members of the body politic) until we finally realized that the life of man as a citizen and a social and economic being must be supplied with blood from this heart which was not thought of in this new way?

For a long time Lutheranism particularly (in Germany at any rate) failed to break through to this insight, but rather left these areas of life to themselves. It did this on the basis of a badly misunderstood doctrine of the two kingdoms. It acted as if this doctrine means that God is interested only in the realm of the spiritual and religious, whereas in the kingdom on the left, in the kingdom of the world, the autonomy of the particular practical areas should prevail, in other words, that here the principle of art for art's sake applies and also the law that political matters can be dealt with only politically and economic matters can be handled only economically. In this respect even the Confessing Church failed, not only when the state attacked the preaching of the Word of God (and the church began to exert a brave opposition, since this was something that directly touched the "heart" and was therefore encroaching upon its province!), but also when the state solved the Jewish question in the most horribly brutal way and delivered the mentally ill and retarded to "euthanasia." Here, apart from a few exceptions, there was silence. For, after all, were not these "political" questions which were not the concern of the church? Were not these matters of the "political" extremities, whereas the church was charged only with the care of the heart?

Thus the split, the dichotomy, the separate existence of the house of life and the house of doctrine side by side was even given theological sanction and the doctrine of the two kingdoms had to take the blame for being the cause of this dichotomy of the Christian life.[2] Warning voices, like that of Dietrich Bonhoeffer, went unheard.

Even the New Testament repeatedly speaks of this vicious dichotomy of the devout man and the preacher. Once one sees this problem one finds it everywhere, from the Gospels to the Epistle of James. We need only to think of the story of the Good Samaritan. The priest and the Levites (in other words, the preachers!) kept clear of the man who had fallen among robbers. They did not help him; for they had to go to Jericho, probably on account of their ministerial duties. And naturally they performed these duties in the name of God! They did not remember that almost always we are unexpectedly meeting our neighbor with his need, that he simply does not fit into our ministerial schedules and therefore requires improvised changes in our plans. But these two clerics did not relate this man, so fortuitously encountered, with God; only their professional schedules had anything to do with God. And they were unaware, or did not want to be aware, that the very thing that this God required of them was this willingness to change their plans, this spontaneous response to need. Perhaps there was a note in their date book: "Evening, Jericho, talk on brotherly love." And who would doubt that they had prepared for this talk, carefully, with prayer, and in the commitment of their hearts! But when this actual, concrete neighbor suddenly lay at their feet, they passed by on the other side. They did so because they wanted to

avoid the association that might arise between their *talk* on brotherly love and this concrete *case*. They simply helped things along a
bit in order to keep the two realms (the sermon in the pulpit and
real life) separated from each other. Was this the reason why the
sermon that night turned out to be rather flat and pallid? Was
that why the listeners said to themselves, "Perfectly correct—but
what has it got to do with my problems and my life"? This objective contradiction between what I teach and the way I live—this is
hypocrisy in the fullest sense of the word. And the demonic thing
about it is that this hypocrisy can go hand in hand with subjective
honesty, indeed, with kind, good-natured unconsciousness of anything wrong. The trouble is that then people stop accepting
anything he says and they say he can't be believed (though subjectively he is perfectly honest!). They sense that actually he is
living *alongside* of his message, that he has a plurality of passions,
and that, as Kierkegaard would say, he does not have "the purity
to will *one* thing."

So if our preaching has lost life and vitality compared with that
of earlier generations, if indeed it is almost dead, it is not because
we are less skillful rhetorically or mentally duller and stuffier than
our fathers, but rather because of this dichotomy in our existence.
The fault lies in a pathological condition in our spiritual life; it is
the problem of "numbness in the extremities." One is reminded
here of Martin Kähler's pulpit prayer: "Cause my mind to fear
whether my heart means what I say."[3]

The Pathology of Spiritual Existence

There may also be an empirical example of the opposite of all that
we have said. Alongside of the miserable examples of preaching
which we have described there are many other instances in which
it is possible to find a receptiveness and a willingness to listen. The
Word which is credibly preached does not return void even in our
day, but comes back laden with souls which have found in it

fulfillment and peace. But a more careful analysis of these favorable examples would also reveal certain inner situations of the potential hearer. If I see aright, people today are not generally asking the question: "Where shall I learn to believe?" In order to ask that question, a person would already have to know by and large what faith is and what it could mean for his own life. People are rather asking, "Where can I find credible witnesses?" I believe that hitherto Protestantism has given far too much thought to faith and far too little to the problem of credibility.

Credibility has to do with the relation of the faith to the person and thus with the question whether a person is really practicing his faith. It is not a matter of whether a person "is" in earnest about it; for who would dare to impugn the seriousness of any earnest witness? No, it is rather a question whether he really practices his faith.

We have seen what this involves. It is not a question of his being the "picture of a saint," as Luther said, and a morally perfect person. He who wished to be or perhaps even imagined himself to be such a thing would by that very token discredit his message of the acceptance of sinners! No, it is rather a question of whether he himself lives and exists in the house of his teaching and preaching. The question of credibility is therefore a question of an existential fact and not of a mental and emotional state; it is not a "psychological" question. Therefore what we are dealing with here is a genuine theme of theology and not with spiritual snooping or the competence of such a dubious province as the psychology of religion.

In this deeper sense, however, the question of the credibility of the witness cannot be ignored. I would even venture to say that today all the really vital questions that touch the depths of existence enter man's consciousness through the medium of persons in whom these questions are, as it were, incarnated. People are not avidly curious about salvation, for example, and you will never hear Luther's question, "How can I find a gracious God?" in a restaurant or a pub. But people are curious to know what a man looks like (and what he looks like inside) who himself lives by a message of salvation, a man who is otherwise just like "you and me," so that I cannot simply explain away his "religiousness" by saying that he must have a different or deviant psychic constitution. People may not want to have a title of nobility, but they are interested in how the nobility live in their families and in their castles. One could search for illustrations of this very serious circumstance even in the most trivial areas.

The inquisitive question of how and what the witness lives by and how his message affects his real life is the psychological form in which the question of credibility manifests itself concretely. And in this sense one may say that the question of credibility points to one of the deepest longings of our time. We are surrounded by legions of "functionaries," propagandists, and paid purveyors of opinion, and nobody knows what they think in their personal and private lives—whether they be political or economic propagandists. One always has the rather macabre impression of being exposed, not to a real conviction, but to a skillfully practiced method of influencing people. Thus a politician who sits with a small circle of friends with a glass of beer and a cigar after having delivered a demagogic speech that rang with conviction can say: "Now, if you want to hear my *personal* opinion. . . ." And a high government official is even capable of dropping an aside in his speech (with a kind of conciliatory irony): "If I were not a secretary but had my own opinion. . . ." Hardly anybody knows any more what the other person "really" thinks because he is animated by remote control and is usually a ventriloquist whose voice sounds like someone else's.

So in a time when we are all accustomed to the functionary's ventriloquism there is simply no sense in using a particular kind of pulpit tone or a strained solemnity in order to indicate even by one's tone of voice that one is moving in sacred heights and in the precincts of ultimate earnestness, and that one is therefore elevated above the misty flats of the secular slaves of opinion. These solemn, elevated signs are of no help at all, since they are also erected on the flats. Saint Joan in her most ecstatic moments could not have spoken more ecstatically than the hired housewife model on television who, confronted by soap powder, utters the visionary words: "The whitest white I ever saw in my life!" It is like looking into the seventh heaven. How could the transport of such a vision ever be excelled phonetically by a witness in the pulpit? And even the solemn tremolo has long since been taken over by the psycho-strategists and the advertising experts. The organ itself has become a favorite means of producing sound effects in kitsch-films to play upon the special nerves that control solemnity. For many people, who want a church funeral, but are not at all interested in the content of the message, the thing no longer works either. All these sacral, or better, pseudo-sacral, tones have long since cropped up in the margarine ads and the sports pages. "After long inner struggle with changing taste," it was stated at a recent food convention, "the housewife has won her way through to a new, definitely German, low-fat cheese-consciousness." One can almost hear in that sentence the ring of Martin Luther's dictum at Worms: "Here I stand, I cannot do otherwise." This raises "cheese-consciousness" to the level of a conviction and makes it a *status confessionis*. And on the sports page I find this utterance: "After the sixth goal which the HSV rammed in on him, Franz-Joseph Zieberg, the Primasens outside right, made no secret of his despair. Matischak, the wonderfully blessed, is dangerous. . . ." The charismatic outside right—it has come to that! We can no longer contend with that kind of competition by merely cultivating solemnity. For a long time now we have had soccer "congregations" and margarine "liturgies." In the deceitful atmosphere of our time we can speak of the Unconditioned only by explaining quite soberly, dispassionately, and realistically the matter we are concerned with, speaking a very natural language in an almost conversational tone. By the very fact that we do *not* speak in any way out of the ordinary we make it clear that the *content* of what we say is different, that God is the "wholly Other."

This age of alienated personality has an unbounded yearning for credibility and a man's "own tone." People are ready to listen to and take seriously even the most odd and strange things, given the situation where a man who is to be taken seriously, himself believes and practices what he believes. Indeed, there are cases in which a person can become world famous through his credibility supply *because* it is such an extravagant exception. Many people do not know that Albert Schweitzer is a great artist and a creative theologian, or at least only a few know what this means. But the fact that he gave up a notable career in the realm of European culture in order to go into the jungle and lance the disgusting abscesses of sick natives in Africa—this has a tremendous fascination, even among those who regard the mission itself to be out-of-date and Lambaréné as a dubious example of hygiene. But the man must be worth believing if he practices his convictions. As we said, a man can become world famous through this simple fact of credibility! So rare is it and so great is the yearning for that kind of witnessing.

Have we not become unbelievable and unconvincing in our Christian preaching—not in the penultimate but in the ultimate dimension—because our preaching no longer reaches people, because it is boring and colorless? If this is so, and I believe it is, then the trouble with preaching lies deep in our actual spiritual condition, in a pathological condition of our Christian existence. Then it does not lie in the fact that the church is in an unfortunate state of competition with all the other appeals and interests in the midst of a world stuffed to the ears with prosperity. Then it does not lie in sociological conditions, such as the changing structure of society which has shifted the center of existence away from personal environment and thus away from the local congregation into the world of work. Then it also does not lie in the fact that the church has lagged behind the spirit of the times and neglected scientific and intellectual progress—as a great deal of shallow popular literature would have us believe.

It is as if the church had sent out a whole host of reconnaissance troops to search out the causes of the trouble with preaching: diagnosticians of the spirit of the times, avant-gardists of every kind, depth psychologists, sociologists (above all, sociologists), experts in mass psychology, clever boys who know how to get at people, publicity men, advertising technicians, and many others. Now it cannot be denied that all of these experts have found some things that are out of order and that here and there the dust of centuries flies up where they have appeared and begun to poke around. But all these solemn analysts seem to me to be like a doctor who discovers a wart or an infected tonsil, but overlooks the rampant carcinoma. As long as we have not conquered the "sickness unto death," which is seated in our unconvincing Christian existence and nowhere else, all the secondary remedies are meaningless and restricted to very innocuous symptom-therapy.

The Intellectual Demand of Preaching

In order to be just, there is, of course, one thing that dare not be overlooked and that is that, quite apart from this existential sickness, the preacher is confronted with a tremendously difficult task which is sufficient to overwhelm him. I do not hesitate to assert that preaching, even from the point of view of a pure job of work, is one of the greatest intellectual tasks that can be expected of a man. When I prepare a lecture, I have to master the material and put it in proper order. In doing so I do not need to enter into any great pedagogical deliberations as to how to present it. After all, I shall be speaking to properly trained persons and my audience is homogeneous in structure. Besides, I can take my time. What I do not get done today I can present in my next lecture and at the same time build upon what I have said before. I can also do something which cannot be done in a book; I can talk "off the cuff," in "rough copy" as it were. I can conduct an experiment in thought and send up a trial balloon. If my experiment fails to hit the mark, I can change my course or withdraw what I said. After all, I am talking to the same people and it makes no difference.

How different the situation is in preaching, however, and what a complex mass of operations need to be mastered and forced into a unity! I have before me an ancient text, which needs to be made to speak to this present day. In order not to fall into the shabby trick of giving the impression of being close to the present merely by capitalizing on the external appeal of this text (during the bombing raids in the last war one had only to read parts of the Revelation of John to trigger the shuddering sense of a seeming contemporaneity), I must know what the text meant in its day and what Isaiah, for example, really intended to say in the moment he uttered it. I have to do a great deal of historical and philological work if the thing is going to be real. I also need to work my way through the problems which have been raised by the historico-critical study of the Bible. For the people who were and are leaders in this study were not, apart from some exceptions, out to make the preacher's task harder, but rather to make it easier. In so far as they were theologically and not merely historically interested in the Scriptures, they were, after all, concerned to make it possible honestly to accept and appropriate the text and honestly to become contemporaneous with it. "Honestly" here means that they started with the conviction that the Bible dare not simply be recited, but rather must be interpreted, that is, the statements which were conditioned by the time in which they were uttered must be listened to so intensely and their proclamatory content so clearly determined that they become transparent for a message that reaches me here and now through the text. "Honestly" means that they also started with the conviction that these kerygmatic affirmations of the text are embedded in forms conditioned by the time in which they were uttered, which we do not need to believe along with the affirmations, but are to be recognized and therefore relativized as mere *media* of the affirmations. Thus the creation story, for example, is naturally embedded in the medium of a pre-Copernican cosmology. In order to believe in God the Creator we do not need to submit to the perverse compulsion to believe also in the obsolete cosmological medium of the message of creation.

Historico-critical study of the Bible therefore provides material for honest appropriation and contemporization. But this material requires to be worked through. And in every new text and therefore in every new sermon it compels the preacher afresh to face the task of making it relevant and timely.

And yet what happens in the pulpit must not turn out to be a lecture on Bible problems and certainly it must not remain that. On the contrary, I must deliver the *message* of this text to people living today. And therefore I must know these people; I must know at what point they raise questions, so that I can "latch on" to these questions, and I must know where they do *not* have questions, so that I must first stir them up to ask the pertinent questions. I must know whether they feel safe and secure, in order that I may shake them, or whether they are troubled with anxiety, that I may be able to comfort and encourage them.

Here are a few old ladies from the old folks' home. They cannot be reached with the intellectual problems that perhaps are of extreme concern to me. They are afraid of loneliness, of death, and they cherish a few tender memories. What shall I aim at with this text when I talk to *them?*

There are the young people who still have their life before them. Some of them have already faced the question of the meaning of life. Others have minds that are stuffed with a mélange of images garnered from television and the picture magazines. An "idea" would never catch them, at most perhaps a little story would. And all these young people without exception are afraid— afraid that they will miss something that life has to offer. For they know, in an altogether unreflected way, that youth is transient and in the end life too, and therefore that time is irreversible. How shall I talk to them about death and eternity? The appeal to fear of dying will certainly not draw their attention. For nobody ever considers that tomorrow he will be run over or die of appendicitis. But perhaps I could speak to them about death by saying: You are all thinking about death, even though you imagine that it will not catch you until you are eighty-four. (After all, do not the statisticians, who are perfectly trustworthy, tell us that life expectation is constantly growing higher?) You *are* counting on death, simply because you are afraid of missing something, simply because as you race down the track of life you are constantly breaking through tapes, behind which you can never return—until you come to the last tape . . .

Thus as a preacher I am involved in an unending dialogue with those to whom I must deliver my message. Every conversation I engage in becomes at bottom a meditation, a preparation, a gathering of material for my preaching. I can no longer listen disinterestedly even to a play in a theater without relating it to my pulpit. Does not what the playwright says keep giving me information concerning where this man stands to whom I owe my message? Is it not a fragment of a great confession? Thus life in all its daily involvements becomes for me a thesaurus in which I keep rummaging, because it is full of relevant material for my message.

But then I must establish the contact between all this and my text. And then I must express it in such a way that the intellect will be stimulated to think, the will mobilized, the conscience aroused, and the emotions engaged. For after all, my message is one that concerns not only all men but also the *whole* man: the man of feeling, the man of intellect, the man of will, and the far larger contingent of those who are a mixture of all three. Must not the very focus and goal of my sermon be such that it addresses all of these dimensions? And will not the dock workers go away empty if in my sermon I have in mind only the shipowners or the schoolteachers? And will not the county judge say: "He did not take me into account today," if I think only of the bum who happens to drop in from the tenderloin?

But how foolish (because far too Herculean) it would be to attempt to reach all these disparate goals at the same time by means of such strategic considerations! Is there not a level in man which is the same in all, that level where he is desperate and lonely, despairing of the meaning of existence, but also where he loves his children, cherishes his fondest wishes, and hopes for the fulfillment of his dreams? Is there not a dimension where all men are identical and homogeneous? How could I ever find it except through love which makes it possible to understand?

But is this love which is so indispensable to preaching always at my command? After all, I too have my fits of rage over the blaring portable radio in my neighbor's garden, I too have my moments of depression and feelings of envy, and often my heart is so glutted with them that there is hardly any room left in the inn of the inner man for love and loving understanding of others. But then all these ponderings of method and goals by which I seek to reach the conscience, feelings, will, and mental level of my hearers are good for nothing at all. For without love, everything I say, no matter how ingeniously worked out it may be, becomes a noisy gong and a clanging cymbal.

In that case, I may well be a clever manipulator and eloquent rhetorician, but there will be something in the tone of my voice that gives me the lie. In one way or another it will come out that I am incredible, not worth believing (there it is again!), and that I am a man without love, who is not living in the house of his words.

The fact is that a preacher is constantly betraying himself. When we meet a druggist, we do not necessarily note whether he loves or hates, whether he dispenses his pills with delight, or whether he is eating out his heart in envy and care. The sales talk goes on its routine way. But with a preacher it soon comes out whether he has come to terms with himself or not. And the thoughts that bicker and grumble in his heart become voices that shout from the housetops. What the druggist thinks does not undermine the words with which he recommends this or that cough medicine; but the preacher, by the state of his soul, can belie the words which have been committed to him, no matter how well chosen and well disposed they are as he utters them.

Therefore the preparation of a sermon also requires a continuing exercise of an inner, spiritual order. And above all it requires an exercise, a training in love, and hence a work (yes, a "work") which includes the whole man. He must really settle a rift in his marriage, a loss of trust in relationship to his children, the bad situation with his fellow minister, and he must learn to carry out this loving understanding existentially in order not to contradict himself and remain convincing, indeed, in order to be able to reach his hearers at all.[4]

What hard work all this is—but also what promises are given to it! No one would assert that it is easy.

And then, finally, it must be ordered speech. It must be clearly thought out and given a well-ordered structure. It must have movement, gradations, plateaus, and pauses. And when an unusually "high" thought is introduced, it must be so embedded in the whole line of thought that the simple listener will not lose the thread. And all this must be accomplished within a definite period of time counted in minutes. And it must really constitute a whole, for someone may be present today who will never come back again and I must give him his emergency rations.

Where is the man who can accomplish all this and who among those who are faced with this enormous assignment does not despair of accomplishing it? (But do those who sit in the pews or those who hear about it secondhand ever give it a thought?) The only man who can assume such a bold and hazardous task is one who is convinced that he need not bear the responsibility for its success and that Another is there interceding for him. He knows that not he but only the Spirit of God himself is able to reach and open the hearts of his hearers. And only to the degree that he is assured of this will he mount the pulpit consoled and strengthened. But even this faith in the miracle of the Spirit can be secured only through practice. It can become a deep, sustaining power only by the exercise of prayer and through one's own listening to the message of the text which is being preached. But this again demands the "whole man."

The Preacher as a Helpless Soloist

And yet, how helpless is this "whole man" if he is only a soloist! It is a question whether the rather obvious impotence of preaching today does not stem from the fact that it has become the utterance of soloists for whom these necessary intellectual and spiritual prerequisities of preaching must always remain out of reach.

Time and again it has been my personal experience that hardly ever do we arrive at such vital, searching, and yet thematically broad discussions as when we talk over with others a text which is to be the basis of a sermon. Even common engagement in the task of interpretation is a stimulating thing, and the question of how the message is to be expressed leads us through far-flung and very exciting landscapes of human life.

To be sure, this should not be merely a matter of discussions with experts and specialists, but rather of consultation with those who will also be the hearers of the sermon, and therefore with "laymen." In this concern they have a function similar to that of a citizen who sits with a professional judge in the disposition of a case of law. With their criteria and different approach to the question, they constitute a salutary corrective to a point of view which may be professionally and objectively proper but is also constricted. To that extent the theological and spiritual exchange with laymen is a healing spring for all the problems we face in preaching. Because the "average men of the world" represent a living and vital point of contact, they make unnecessary what is often a sterile theorizing about the question of where the other person stands and what questions I must address myself to in order to reach him. This becomes superfluous because, after all, the other person is right there with his questions and problems.

Not only in his preaching but also in his scholarly work one can see whether a theologian has found his question among "laymen" and cultivates a professional (not merely a general cultural or social) exchange of ideas with them. I believe that the reason why such broad areas of our theology today are so unfruitful and why there are so many barren thinkers in a time which is ripe for harvest is that the theologians are not doing much more than providing each other with problems and solutions. Then further work can consist only in a refinement of what is already given, a chasing of an already polished surface. And the next one can distinguish himself only if he possesses a more delicate micrometric screw which will show a still more exact segment of the already projected and focused picture. It is only a matter of more precise adjustments and hardly of new ideas.

"I am constantly reminded," says Heinz Zahrnt with graphic irony, "of the spectacle of two men on a scaffold at the top of a cathedral spire, violently quarreling over whether the last bit of ornament should be turned to the right or the left, both of them looking as if they were about to plunge to the street. Down below people stand looking up and have no idea what it is all about. And because they do not understand it, they turn away shaking their heads."

This esoteric scholasticism of the professionals—it is even more intense when members of the same theological school get together —is a long way from that which agitates the average devoted Christian or a neo-pagan who is interested in religion. These knacks and skills of an overbred logic are far removed from sound common sense. And because he feels helpless, he avoids any such contact—unless you regard the definite feeling of being near something weird as being a form (albeit negative) of contact.

If there were a comparative or a superlative of the word "sterile," I should think it would have been reached where this intraprofessional concern is concentrated upon a relatively diminutive subject matter and then leads to the examination of every single letter, so that one can hardly see the forest of the message for the trees of letters. The New Testament, that "little booklet" (as Adolf Schlatter called it), has repeatedly been subjected to this kind of horse doctoring. A great many New Testament scholars remind me of a gigantic ballet dancing on a saucer, and what is more, always repeating the same figures. One can imagine what is broken and ruined in the process.

A great classical scholar told me not long ago about his listening to an inaugural lecture delivered by an equally eminent New Testament scholar. It was not, it is true, a disquisition on the particle *"de"* in the writings of Paul, but it must have been a similar microscopical problem. The classical scholar was simply beside himself with astonishment that this learned man should have concentrated his sweaty exertions upon such a detail and he said: "Where would the likes of us end up if we were to subject Homer and Aeschylus and Xenophon to such pinpoint borings. These gentlemen have too little material to work on!"

The last diagnosis may, of course, have been wrong. The reason for the pinpoint boring was not in the alleged minuteness of the material, but rather in the narrow range of the questions applied to it. It lay in the fact that the professionals of that particular school had sunk their teeth in a particular problem and no longer saw anything else. Perhaps the man might have been helped, if he had listened to the questions of a wide-awake Christian, even a Bible-believing layman. The most fruitful theological questions always come from outside of theology. Only here do we have the polarity that generates sparks.

Theologians, however, tend to press faith in the Virgin Birth too far when, as many of them do, they appear to cherish the illusion that *problems* too are produced by parthenogenesis, that is to say, in the monologue carried on by the professional clique. This scholastic pond must necessarily turn brackish if it has no inlet or outlet.

Let me offer here a tribute to the manes of the great Schleiermacher (to use a phrase which this master used with regard to Spinoza). True, we join issue with him, we oppose him at many points, but not in everything. And yet no one would deny that there is not a single theologian since the Reformation who can hold a candle to him for depth, systematizing power, and continuing influence. Why? Because he did not simply go on spinning old threads and threshing the empty straw, but rather found his questions in a living dialogue with his time, and out of this polarity there came to him ideas which in many different variations are still our own problems.

The Dualism between Preacher and Professor

We are in danger of becoming a church of parsons, which is to say, a church without laymen (even though here and there they may still fill the churches). And we are also in danger of becoming a theology without the church, a church without theology, because both are talking past each other. The theologians, many of them, do not remember that it is their task to provide equipment for preachers (and, what is more, to preachers who have to preach to *laymen*). The laymen on their part are simply bewildered by theological logic-chopping and they distrust it. The church administrators feel that theology is leaving them in the lurch and they muddle through *in rebus theologicis* in their own way. Again the professionals turn up their noses at this and chafe at the pragmatic dilettantism of ecclesiastical bureaucrats, these *terribles simplificateurs* who duck the embarrassing questions posed, for example, by the existential interpretation of the Bible merely to prevent any sand from getting into the routine grinding of the apparatus.

So each goes on spinning his own thread and the result is an intrachurch variant of our pluralistic society. But while this pluralistic structure of social life seems to work, after a fashion, in the "world"—for there people are tolerant and the problems do not cut so close to the quick—in the church it leads to the sterile coexistence of groups or to the mutually mistrustful antagonism of people who are convinced they are right.

Meanwhile the Body of Christ is further and further rent asunder. We moan, not altogether without reason, that it is the confessions and denominations that constitute such a rift in the Body of Christ. But far worse is the ineluctable dualism between the pulpit and the professor's lectern. As between the confessions people are beginning to speak to each other across the dividing lines and increasingly brothers are beginning to recognize and sometimes to embrace each other. There seems, however, to be hardly a bridge across the gulf between the pulpit and the professor's lectern. And despite all the lay movements, church congresses, and evangelical academies, there are only a few miserable foot bridges over the chasm between the clergy and the laity. This is where the most blood flows from that wounded Body.

In these days when my Hamburg faculty of theology is completing its first decade I remember with gratitude that here every member of the faculty also preaches. We have sworn to raise this banner in order to help to bridge this chasm in our little corner. Not all of us would say that preaching is in our line and sometimes it becomes somewhat professorial. But this does not matter. We climb the walls of Jerusalem and shout it into the land wherever we see the bleeding wounds and the yawning chasms.

Unwittingly the scope of my discussion has broadened. At first I was concerned only to recommend that preachers should discuss their texts with laymen in order to gain the spark of stimulation from this polarity with them. But we have seen that this question belongs in the context of a larger problem, namely, in the whole relationship of theology to the laity, or one might say with the Reformers, in the context of the universal priesthood of believers. Anybody who speaks a great deal about this (and the fact is that we do speak a great deal about it) may actually be denying it (and the fact is that we do deny it).

But all these broad analyses of the intellectual and the spiritual conditions of our time are useless if we do not indicate at least a small area of realizable action which can be tackled directly. And discussion of our preaching with laymen seems to me to be one of these areas. Here, it seems to me, is the source of power for a revival—and not only a revival of preaching itself, which could thus be rescued from the fate of the monologue and the solo. It could also be a source of power for the laymen. For they are in peril of spiritual death, not merely because they are compelled to listen to dead and boring sermons and thus remain spiritually undernourished, but above all because even where there is vital preaching they are largely obliged to play the role of a mere "audience," which quite passively allows itself to be homiletically sprinkled.

I have seen in American Sunday Schools how it is possible to get out of the infernal role of an "audience" and get into dialogue. When I say this I do not mean to idealize the American Sunday School and the preaching which it fructifies. All this too has its drawbacks and we shall speak of them later. But where among men and in this still unfinished aeon are there no drawbacks! The German preacher often begins in heaven and never comes down to our living earth. The American preacher, just because he remains in vital contact, begins with downright earthly life and its social and psychological problems and, often enough, never reaches heaven. Be that as it may, there is life here, perhaps sometimes a lot of "machine tending" too; but the deadly boredom and the curse of merely doctrinal correctitude is not so common as it is among us.

We ought to begin this dialogue with laymen. This, in brief, is what I wanted to say.

The preacher ought also to study the great masters and see how they approached their work spiritually and solved the practical problems of preaching. The reason why I attempted to make German preachers familiar with Spurgeon was that I consider him one of these great masters and also because he has so well expressed the "what" and the "how" of preaching in the form of experiential communication and basic axioms.[5]

The Dictatorship of the Listeners

There is, of course, one small reservation that I must make here. I said that every sermon must grow out of a dialogue with the listeners and that the preparatory discussion with laymen should symbolically represent, or better, prefigure this dialogue. But this must not imply that the preacher dare to make himself dependent upon the needs of his particular hearers. Generally these hearers of his are—sociologically speaking—only a very partial selection which by no means represents the proportions of our whole society. (To judge what these proportions are one would have to study the audience in a movie house when certain films are shown.) Mostly they are old ladies, middle-class citizens, people living on pensions and private means, and children, in short, people who live, as it were, "unhistorically," who do not live where people who are active by nature and age live their lives, where things are thick and the pressures are great.

Why this is so, we shall discuss later; but we may say at least one thing here. This make-up of the average congregation dare not, in my opinion, be attributed to the general secularization of life, but is rather connected with the form of preaching itself, which is likewise "unhistorical" or is—as we shall point out later —docetic in character. In no case, then, dare the preacher make himself dependent upon his congregation of this kind of hearers, even though this would seem the obvious thing for him to do. Should he not, as we have said, live in dialogue with them, and does he not owe his message precisely to those who are actually present? No, this is not the case. God sent his Son because he loved the "world" (and not merely a scanty and one-sided segment of the world). He desires "all men" to come to the knowledge of the truth (not merely the pensioners and old ladies, however much they too are loved and belong to the category of "all men"). The preacher must also address those who are not present, though he certainly will not take this "must" to mean that he should berate the inhabitants of an old folks' home with fulminations about sexual immorality and dance-crazy youth.

If the preacher makes himself dependent upon the given hearers in his congregation, he will be sucked into a vicious circle. Old ladies love sentiment and feeling, and they want no problems; they hardly know what to make of it if one tells them what the gospel can mean for the great conflicts of life and the bitter ensnarements of passion. But if I keep silent on these themes because of my given listeners, I shall perhaps win the hearts of the old ladies with my homiletical lullaby, but then the others will certainly stay away. Because the old ladies are present (and I beg you not to interpret this as a sarcasm directed at these respectable mothers and grandmothers!) I begin to speak only for old ladies; and therefore in future only old ladies come while the others are frightened away. What youth would venture into a group of gray-heads? And who would not take to flight when what he hears is also addressed only to grayheads?

The preacher dare not fall into this vicious circle. He must speak for those who are not present *as if* they were present. Then they too will come. This is a prescription which has been confirmed many times in practice. But even if this were not the case, he would be obliged to do it nevertheless, simply because his preaching cannot be addressed to any but those who are addressed by the gospel itself. But the gospel is addressed to the *world*. This thesis also constitutes the heart of the program of a "nonreligious" or "worldly" interpretation of the Christian message, as set forth, for example, by a man like Dietrich Bonhoeffer.

The Decay of the Language of Preaching

Nevertheless, in our investigation of the crisis of preaching we must delve still deeper, and when we do so we come up with the problems of the language of preaching. We have already seen how incredible and hollow it becomes when it simply employs the conventional vocabulary without reworking it. Then its generalized timelessness never gets under people's skins. It fails to challenge me, it has nothing to do with my life, and from a psychological point of view it functions only as narcotic boredom.

What happens here can be understood only if we give some thought to two considerations—which, if you want to call them that, are problems of the philosophy of language.

The first consideration can be very general. Like everybody else, the preacher uses the given stock of words which is contained in our language. The fact is that there is no special religious vocabulary. Here we are not discussing glossolalia, speaking in tongues, in which a kind of ecstasy explodes in inarticulate sounds, a phenomenon which receives very critical mention in the New Testament.[6]

Every word we use carries with it a certain definite intellectual content. Therefore words undergo a kind of ideological conversion when they are employed in the service of proclamation. This can be observed in the New Testament itself, for example in the way it takes over the Stoic term "Logos" and uses it in the prologue of the Gospel of John. Here the term "Logos" had first to shed its Stoic meaning-content. The term had, so to speak, to repent and be baptized before it could be used kerygmatically. Also the term "righteousness" or "justice," as Paul, for example, uses it, has been radically transformed, compared with the corresponding term in Plato. Naturally, in their origin and original significance these terms had a very definite affinity with that which the witnesses would later express by means of these words. Otherwise they would not have chosen these particular terms but rather others! Only *these* terms were suitable as material into which the new signification and content could be stamped.

But then it soon becomes apparent that the ancient gods who were immured in the temple of these words (so that this temple was able to provide building stones for the new message) burst out of their prison and became "virulent" again. And again this can be seen in what happened to the term "Logos." Hardly had it been tamed and recoined in the Gospel of John when its original meaning celebrated its gleeful resurrection in the Apologists of the second century. In Stoic philosophy "Logos" meant the Cosmic Reason, and to that extent it was the goal of all philosophers. But the philosophers were able to pursue this Cosmic Reason only because it possessed, as it were, a foothold in the mind of individual philosophers. Only because their eyes had a sunlike nature could they see the sun of the Logos. Their individual reason was an offshoot (*logos spermaticos*) of the Cosmic Reason. So the Apologists of the Church sought to reinterpret Christ in terms of this ancient Logos concept. Thus they reinterpreted, not the Logos, but Christ; for them the Logos was the normative standard. This they did by saying: "Christ is the Cosmic Reason. He is therefore the fulfillment of all that was fragmentarily attained in your philosophers. So when you become Christian you need not be any different from what you were before. Faith need not be an intellectual offense; rather it leads you to the fullness of that which is only partially accessible to your own intellectual initiative."

Thus the old content was revived and it proceeded to absorb the kerygma until it actually ceased to exist. Consequently, the struggle between Christ and the gods goes on. After each twilight of the gods a new day of the gods seems to dawn.

The church must therefore take care when it speaks and uses words. Therefore it must always take care, since after all, it is always speaking. And it always speaks in terms of the given language, employing its words and, as it were, baptizing them. But then it must reckon with the fact that these words will apostatize and that their former meanings will regenerate themselves.

What happens is much the same as with the Trojan horse. This wooden monster was drawn into the holy city of Ilion by quite innocent people; but suddenly the trapdoor in the wooden belly opened, Agamemnon and Menelaus stepped out, and turned the Trojan flank from inside the city. There is also such a trapdoor in the wooden horse of language which has been drawn into the holy Ilion of the church. And suddenly the Stoics, Plato, Hegel, and Heidegger step out of it.

These fifth-column episodes have occurred time and time again in the history of Christianity. This was the case, for example, in the process which Adolf Harnack called the "Hellenization of Christianity." It is true that the Greek terms for "psyche," "body," "flesh," and "spirit" acquired a wholly new meaning in the New Testament. They were baptized. But the Greek vocabulary soon brought about a reanimation of the ancient Greek meanings, and these terms were then interpreted in accord with the *original* anthropology from which they sprang. And since Hellenism was rather hostile to the body, Christianity, which employed this loaded term for the body, then became hostile toward the body and sex. And the ancient term for "soul" soon saw to it that the doctrine of the immortality of the soul reoccupied a place in Christian thought, even though it had originally been conquered by the message of the Resurrection.

Every one of us knows how miserably we still have to struggle today with these reanimated relics of the past and especially with pseudo-Christian hostility to the body. We must therefore take care that our baptized terms are not understood in the sense of their unbaptized state and that people will not hear in them something completely different from what they mean. And here I am optimistic enough to cherish the hope that the preacher himself is not a secret Hellenist, Idealist, or existentialist and hence that he well knows the meaning of Christian terms in contrast with their original pagan meanings or their regenerated or degenerated neo-pagan significations.

Indeed, our caution in the use of terms must go even further. That is to say, we must by no means conclude that specifically Christian words, like "sin" or "grace," for example, or even the word "Christ," are exempt from these dangers. For even these words are not received in a pure state, but are rather freighted with a history which has often manipulated and altered their meaning. Have we not gone through times like the period of Rationalism, times of ethical reinterpretation of Christianity, which have produced a complete moralization of the concept of sin? Where is the average person today who, when he hears the word "sin," really hears what the New Testament meant by that word? For whom today does this word still say that here man is being addressed at the point of his resistance and opposition to God, that this means man in his will to assert his autonomy, his insistence that everything centers in man, his incredible passion for security, his lostness in preoccupation with the moment and that which is tangible and immediately at hand? And yet all this *must* be heard when we hear the word "sin," if for no other reason than to understand that it is possible for a sinner to be at the same time an example of moral perfection and that he need by no means be a criminal, an antisocial, or even a person who lacks seriousness. Were not the Pharisees ethically very respectable people? And yet for Jesus they were more drastic examples of sin than publicans and prostitutes. And the word "Christ" itself? What would really be the result if we were to investigate the exchange value of that term in the psychological substructure of the average man today? What we would come out with would probably be some idea of a fabulously wise man or a perfect human being.

The point is that we need to say what we *mean* by these terms; we dare not throw them at people as supposedly valid coins whose value is immediately recognized. Otherwise we shall all too thoughtlessly reach out for them with the notion that they are perfectly familiar, whereas the truth is that the metal begins to glow and burn only when we have some idea of what these coins really signify.

The necessity of interpretation and the fact that words which are *not* interpreted become meaningless was borne in upon me one time during the Nazi regime as I let my thoughts dwell on this subject. I imagined a demonstration in the Berlin Sportpalast put on by the German Faith Movement with the appropriate anti-Christian agitation. As the hate tirades reached their climax, a Christian in the audience could stand it no longer. He felt that he must stand up and declare himself and he loudly shouted out, "Christ is the Messiah." In the rows of seats in front of him—I imagined—a few people turned around to look with surprise at the interrupter only to turn away again from this presumed zealot and concentrate their attention upon the platform.

But there was another who spoke out somewhat more clearly. He shouted, "Christ is the only Lord and Leader and without him Hitler and all the apostles of this false faith will go to hell." This man was mobbed and torn to pieces, for that exclamation, God knows, "hit home." This was something that could be understood. And the reactions were appropriate. And yet he had done nothing more than the other man had done when he spoke out for the Messiah—except that he had interpreted the term. And that made it living preaching, whereas the noninterpreted word disappeared in a vacuum.

Again and again at Easter services I am shocked by the casual, matter-of-course way in which the news that Christ is risen is taken. Anybody who has really grasped what that means would be rocked in his seat. And at least a few times I have also noted the shaking of the foundations that occurs when a powerful sermon really communicates the meaning of the Easter message. When that message dawns on us we are suddenly surrounded by life, where before we had our mortgaged past at our backs and ahead of us only a future beset with anxieties. Then life suddenly looks different and then a man will also *live* differently. A transvaluation of all values will take place: we will smile in the face of what before made us lose our nerve, and we will learn to fear things which hitherto we desired or considered harmless. But when the same old normal Christian vocabulary is rolled out at Easter, the only reaction of the congregation is to think, "Yes, the usual thing. We've heard it all before. But it's a good thing to have it said again; we need this repetition of the confirmation material *once a year*." And then when in addition there is a long liturgy which does not *complete* the time-bound sermon with that which is supertemporal and unchanging, but is experienced by the congregation merely as some more rehashing of the conventional material, the circle of the obvious, of high-level boredom, is complete.

Obviously, we must interpret these things in our own language in order that they may be understood. I once experimented with students, having them prepare sermons in which the conventional terms like "God," "sin," "grace," etc. did not appear. The words had to be paraphrased. I think this is a good exercise, even though it has importance only as an interim practice. For we should not discontinue the use of these words in the pulpit; all we need is a withdrawal-cure because of the thoughtless use we make of them. We need to learn to overcome the temptation to string together the old words in different variations, because then souls remain underfed and are lost.

Modernity—Veneer or Substance?

Here we are faced with another important realization. We ought not to think (as conventional ministers are wont to do) that anybody who endeavors to achieve a modern colloquial tone in the pulpit is merely making concessions to the "modern world," that he is being opportunistically accommodating in order to curry favor with the wicked man of the world and to take the sting of offense from his message. Naturally, there is this type of cultured abbé who owns a dictionary of quotations, who sprinkles his sermons with references to Franz Kafka and Robert Musil and is constantly displaying his studiousness and his wide reading.

Between these two types—the preacher and interpreter who speaks in modern terms and the modernistic salon-abbé—there runs a very subtle but clear line of demarcation. No one ever characterized this difference quite as aptly as did Martin Kähler when he said: "It is true that Paul said that he wanted to be a Jew to the Jews and a Greek to the Greeks [that is, that he wanted to accommodate to them]. But he refused to be a miracle-worker to the Jews and a 'cultural Christian' to the Greeks." Kähler was indicating that there is such a thing as accommodation motivated by love which seeks to reach the other person by speaking his language, and that alongside of it there may be an accommodation motivated by opportunism which simply agrees with what others say and tells them only what they want to hear. The Jew of that day had a passion for miracles and stupendous interventions from the Beyond, while the Greek intellect itched for wisdom and ingenious wit. To yield and accommodate oneself at this point is indeed a betrayal of the dignity of my mission as a preacher. And the popularity a witness garners in this way does not glorify the Lord but rather crucifies him and merely glorifies the rhetorical opportunist.

But what about that other kind of accommodation, the kind which the witness in the Sportpalast perpetrated when he attacked the people there with familiar, conventional words and conceptions? Here I would say that the more a man speaks in modern terms the more he will be heard. And the more he is heard the greater will be the acceptance *and* the rejection of his message, the more provocative will it be, and the more emphatic will be the decisions and separations that result. Anybody who has attempted this kind of speech will have encountered these reactions in his own experience. When the Word becomes flesh again, that is to say, when it enters into our own time, wearing the dress of the present, the ancient laws of the proclamation of the Word come into play and it becomes apparent that this Word is a divider of spirits and a hammer which breaks the rock in pieces. Then we learn again that "the disciple is not above his master" and that again, as always, discipleship is accompanied by hate and persecution, slander and defamation. Who will dare to accuse of unfaithfulness the man who is "modern" and interprets the message in *this* way?

Actually, the unfaithful witness is the one who simply transmits the conventional and familiar, unchanged and undigested. He is unfaithful, in the first place, because he is lazy. For the labor of interpretation and contemporization, the work of "translation" is grueling work and it is never done without abortive trials and breath-taking risks. For he who dares to carry the Word into our time has given up all chance to retreat into the safey of tradition. He who simply repeats the old phrases takes no risks; it is easy to remain orthodox and hew to the old line. But he who speaks to this hour's need and translates the message will always be skirting the edge of heresy. He, however, is the man who is given this promise (and I really believe this promise exists): *Only he who risks heresies can gain the truth.*

But the conventional preacher is unfaithful, in the second place, because he gives his hearers stones instead of bread—*venerable* stones to be sure, but in this form they cannot be swallowed. And besides, in this way he travels the safest road so as to prevent any unpleasantnesses from arising. Nobody will ever get excited and so nobody will ever be excited against *him* either. The safest advice to give to the man who wants to get through unscathed is to tell him to stick to conventional preaching. Boresomeness para-

lyzes people, but it does not make them angry. And finally even
the demons fall asleep. But he who sleeps commits no sin. Even
when you sleep in church you commit no sin, that is, you don't
flare up, you don't protest, you never say "Ouch," you don't say,
"Crucify him, let his blood be on us and on our children, I will
have nothing to do with this man." Nobody is ever shocked by
lukewarm drip from the pulpit, but that temperature may make
him sick enough to retch.

The man who wants this easy berth as a preacher also becomes
susceptible to a very false consolation when the pews grow empty
(except in places which have grown insensitive to dullness and
stupidity, where the law of inertia has taken over and the habit of
churchgoing outweighs all other impulses). This false consolation
which is sought by the man who is thus deserted is the argument
that it is the offense of the message that drives people out of the
temple, that therefore there must have been some very faithful
preaching to have produced all these empty pews. But all along
the man has been shirking and evading the offense. Not a single
person was offended or upset; nobody protested. It was only boredom that emptied the pews. The Pharisaism and smugness about
such situations is almost unbelievable. I would never have thought
it possible if I had not seen it myself.

Need I still make a special point of the fact that this is not to
say that empty pews are always a symptom of this boresomeness
and Pharisaism? If I were to say this, I should be doing a grave
injustice to many faithful witnesses who are preaching to empty
pews, whether it be that the preacher has provoked a real decision
against his real message, or whether he is working on dry, stony
soil in which nothing seems to grow despite all a man's selfless
and properly executed work.

I can think of those who persevere and do not give up only with
respect and brotherly affection. And I can only say with shame-
faced soberness that I do not know whether I could bear it,
whether I am capable of this degree of faithfulness, of stubborn

faith, and selflessness in the ministry of witness. The world is not worthy of it, one is tempted to say. And it is a great comfort to know that in a world that lives by success and publicity there are such witnesses, who work quietly and without ambition, who go on preaching as sober men in the midst of an inebriated world and never grow weary, men who walk with bruised feet on stony ground, looking for crevices in which to cast the good seed.

The mere fact that they exist is itself a comfort. They serve a Lord who looks, not for success, but for fruit. Perhaps some guiding word which this preacher uttered years ago lingers in the mind of a single listener in his last hour. With that word he will come before the throne of God, and there it will be recognized as a fruit which no human eye ever saw or even regarded as such. In eternity, however, the diagnoses are different.

The Breakdown of Words and Their Revival

I said that there was a second consideration which relates to the problem of the language of preaching. It brings to our notice certain facts which are not confined to the situation of preaching. These facts perhaps have to do with problems that emcumber our whole situation with regard to language and communication—in literature, philosophy, and even in journalism. It may be a rather dubious comfort to know that preaching *too* shares the intellectual lot of its time and is not merely subject to a peculiar and special degeneration of its own. The consolation is dubious, of course, because the proclamation of the eternal Word is not simply subject to general trends, but is itself supposed to set a trend. It is supposed to contain salt, which does not simply lose its saltness when the soil of language threatens to lose its savor; rather it should salt it and preserve it from decay. The way this preservation should come about is simply that it should get out among the words of the poets and thinkers and be mixed with the words that are used at the gas stations, the labs, the newspaper columns, and there set the standards of truth. But this is just what the preaching of that eternal Word seems *not* to be doing. And this is our fault. Our words in preaching are merely sharing the current infirmity of all other words.

(I interrupt here for a moment, for I have just returned from hearing a sermon which by its breath-taking banality has thrown me completely off the track. So many words and nothing said! I observed a lawyer who sat beside me, suffering the same torments that I did. Empty straw, all the clichés that just seemed to flood into the preacher's head! And knowing that it was all pious blather —for the man is by no means stupid—he turned on the rhetorical explosions in order to dispel the boredom by pseudo-dramatizations. If you had been looking at his gestures through a sound-proof glass partition or if it had been possible to observe the phonetic variations between loud and quiet on a recording apparatus, you would have thought this was a Demosthenes displaying the whole range of his oratorical potential. And all the while it was such inflated nothingness that was the more painful simply because it was pumped up, because the man actually *can* speak —and because he obviously had not worked on it at all or perhaps for only a short half hour. I could not help but think of the precision with which even a little juggler on the stage of a provincial variety theater operates, the honest and disciplined work he does, and the offense that would be taken if he showed the slightest sign of sloppiness. Apparently it is possible to handle the Word of God sloppily, but obviously you can't do the same thing with balls. How shocking is the display of slovenliness in this of all places! How this man, with all his probity in other respects, must despise the Word to be capable of dealing with it so sloppily [there really is no other word for it]. For we hear that he is a good organizer and that his bureaucratic affairs seem to be in good order. If he would only devote a fraction of the care he bestows on his organizational work! It is true that this degree of empty loquacity is unusual, but I have all too often observed these signs of slovenliness. Here the salt of speech has lost all its saltness. There is no promise in this kind of thing at all; this is really denial. The trite, hackneyed nullities which he presented and the conventional dogmatic clichés he used to accomplish it—these no longer proclaim anything. Almost physically, I had the odor of death in my nostrils. This is the dying church. And here again it was tormenting to realize that this spiritual putrefaction was not emanating from a tired old man, but that this face whose mouth was uttering these dead and moldy words and phrases was fresh and bright with health. Here the sickness of speech in our time was not merely shared; here it rose to the top of the fever chart. I had to include this experience here because it was such a distressing first-hand illustration of the ideas I have been talking about—and because it is to the point—unfortunately!)

Well, what is this sickness, the infirmity of our language?

It is the novelists and poets—who, after all, must know this and who are quite as familiar with it as the preachers—who have discussed it and confessed that they are the victims of this infirmity. I shall mention here only a few illustrations of what they say.

I think first of the famous "Letter of Lord Chandos" (*Brief des Lord Chandos*) with which Hugo von Hofmannsthal takes leave of the youthful epoch of his writing career.[7] In this letter Hofmannsthal regards himself as being doomed to a great silence because the words no longer support what he wants to say. The "abstract words, which the tongue must naturally employ in order to express any kind of judgment, fell from my lips like moldy mushrooms. . . . Everything crumbled into pieces and the pieces fell apart into further pieces, and nothing would allow itself to be encompassed in a concept. The individual words swam about me, they congealed into eyes that stared at me and I was compelled to stare at them. They are a vortex and it makes me dizzy to look into it, they are constantly revolving and to go through them brings one into nothing but emptiness."[8]

This experience that Hofmannsthal suffered is the experience that puts one to silence, the experience that language has become *untrue*. Once it was true; on the lips of earlier generations language grasped reality. But now it is as if it had become worn out. It is as if the words, having performed their task, are empty of all content. Language once adequately expressed a particular relationship to reality, but now when we, whose relationship to reality has changed, use the same words, they become untrue. They cease to be a means of grasping and comprehending reality; "they stand at bay before things." "Hearsay has swallowed up the world," Hofmannsthal wrote a few years earlier. And also this: "A man would be a writer beyond all the German writers of the last decades if one could say of him that he has the adjectives which are not stillborn and that his rhythms nowhere go against his will."[9] In other words, he used no words which were merely imitative, words which were dead in the very act of speaking them; he would have his "own tone," which, as Hofmannsthal said, "is everything."

Novalis made a similar observation about the death of language: "The meaning of the world. We have stopped short at the letter [that is, the defunct element of speech]. In our preoccupation with the manifestation [one might add: with that which is merely sound] we have lost what is being manifested."[10]

In our own generation Gottfried Benn spoke of the same thing. The poet [unfortunately he does not speak of the preacher!] is an anchorite whose "monological art . . . stands out in sharp relief from the veritably ontological emptiness that hangs over all speech and raises the question whether all language still has any dialogical character in a metaphysical sense. Does it still establish any relationship at all, does it overcome separation . . . or is it nothing more than material for business consultations and otherwise only a symbol of a tragic decay?"[11]

After the World War I, Ernest Hemingway had already observed that in the face of that ghastly event all hitherto existing words had lost their validity and that the only thing we could express with any claim to truth were proper names and the names of streets. But after World War II, which pitched us even deeper into wordlessness. Hermann Broch said of the breakdown of speech:

> We stare at them, they stare at us:
> the eyes, theirs and ours,
> are still capable of looking
> and deceiving themselves into thinking
> that they are seeking human beings.
> Woe, if a man speaks.[12]

Therefore those who are deeply troubled by this debasement and falsity of language seek for alienating surprise effects which will strip it of its mendacity, the falsity of its sham reliability, and allow it again to exert the effect of a shock. Only surprised astonishment over what is here said and which actually communicates reality can be a seal of the genuineness of language. This may take the form of an "unpleasant way of surprising" people, which Novalis called for, or the use of strange words which are rich in sound and associated meanings, of the kind which Gottfried Benn inserts in the midst of a poem, or the studied crudeness with which Bert Brecht disperses the "rotten mysticism" of plush, emotional speech. This alienating surprise effect by which our dead language is again to be made capable of speaking is as it were a response to the fact that language has alienated itself from reality. If the writer (or the preacher) succeeds in raising this sunken reality and bringing it to light, it actually does have this effect of being alienating, surprising, new, and shockingly unexpected. The use of surprising and alienating speech may therefore be a legitimate means of achieving this effect.

Obviously, many preachers have also sensed what the writers and language experts have discovered. They realize that the conventional vocabulary of church language is deceiving or—to express it in psychological terms—that the words "sin" and "grace" no longer "attract" unless they have first passed through the medium of a living human being and have left this human being transformed, so that he himself is a confession and a witness.

Naturally, these words in themselves are not a lie; they are objectively true. But does not objective truth applied to an existential situation become a lie? Was not Kierkegaard right when he said that the truth of the "existing thinker" lies in its *relation* to what he says and not in the objective correctness of what is said? And does not the Johannine Christ point to the same thing when he speaks of people who are "in" the truth and not of people who merely "speak" the alleged truth? No, we dare not say that these *words* are lies; we can only accuse ourselves, who have allowed these worn and debased words to become lies. They are vehicles of a sunken truth. And those who do not lift them up into the light become liars, because they act like possessors of the truth and still do not know why and how they hold it in their hands and pass it on to others.

As we have said, the preacher too may sense all of this, and therefore we can see this grasping for surprise effects in church life too: the desperate recourse to shocking, offensive, coarse, or hyper-modern words or the introduction of jazz and Negro spirituals into the services of worship. This too is intended to serve as a kind of provocative shock, for the solemn organ tones and the conventional hymns threaten to generate the "rotten mysticism" of which Bert Brecht spoke. These lull people to sleep with something which through this medium once broke in upon this world with proclamatory power and excitement, but which has long since been domesticated and has sunk to the level of customary piety. The sharp-pointed spears of what was once relevant proclamation have been swathed with cotton and their impact is hardly felt. But perhaps we shall again recognize their original sharpness if the messages shock and surprise us and do not come to us in the old familiar form.

Clerical Promoters

It is often the young and vital congregations which manifest this need to be provocative. We ought to respect the honest concern and the sensitive conscientiousness which are manifesting themselves here, but we should also clearly understand that every service of worship which sees salvation only in new means of expression and communication is accursed. For then it may be nothing more than an expression of faith in certain *methods* of salvation, by means of which men think they can seize control of God and make the work of the Holy Spirit unnecessary. This would be merely a new variation of the service of the law and an assault upon what the Reformation taught us about justification by faith alone. For here works and methods become means of salvation.

Here everything depends upon our discerning between spirits. There is an honestly disquieted spirit who has come to the shocking realization that the ultimate and liberating truth is to be found in the gospel, but that the conventional means of expression no longer deliver this truth, but rather keep it hermetically sealed in word cells. And this spirit, who has been thus struck by the truth and wounded by its sharp spear, then seeks for new means of expression. This kind of spirit we must welcome.

But there is also another kind of spirit. There is the spirit who is hot for publicity and promotion, the spirit who lusts after expansion and smarts because the machinery of the church goes on running without producing anything, because it no longer "grips," "takes hold," "attracts." He is the homo-faber-spirit who wants to fabricate new mechanisms to rationalize and effectively structure the process of sowing the Word. And in his very pragmatic cogitations he too may arrive at the idea of producing the shock effect. The psycho-strategist also knows that it is possible by this means to lodge hooks in the mind and prevent the familiar and conventional from fecklessly running off without getting under the skin. So he plots new effects and new methods which will produce these effects.

We must warn against these spirits. They are operators who are bent only upon attractive novelties and will not put an end to the unproductive rattling of the ecclesiastical machinery but will only make it run faster. There are enough of these fellows. Mostly they get only casual customers who are attracted by the new window decorations but soon turn away when they find out that the man has no reserves under the counter but has put everything in the show window. Young people especially have a finely developed sense of whether somebody merely wants to "influence" them or whether here is a man who has seen something that hit him and overpowered him and to which he must now bear witness no matter what it costs. They sense whether what is handed out is a synthetic fabrication of novelties or whether this is somebody who is speaking in his "own tone" about something that has come to him in a new and original way.

It is therefore fatuous (and intellectually crude) to ask the summary question in the church: Should we cultivate an unconventional form of speech, should we permit the tone of the streets or of secular culture in the pulpit, should we turn over the organ to the new music and let the jazz orchestras play at our services? We need to test the spirits and determine to what spirit these advocates of the new belong—whether they are men who have been struck by the message and are now bearing witness to that message with new means, or whether they are merely clever fellows who are suffering from their brain waves or liturgical playboys who want to try a new twist. The distinction between old and new is too inadequate. It is a question of the Spirit, who speaks both through the old and the new.

The Language of the Professionals

I cannot emphasize too strongly that I have no wish to abolish the accustomed theological vocabulary and to pose as an iconoclast of the technical language of Christianity. The reference to the odor of decay that clings to the old, worn-out language applies only to the vocabulary which is simply passed on without being worked upon and digested, the vocabulary which shows no sign that it has gone through the medium of a living witness and is therefore brimful of associations with life that has been really experienced. We may also put it this way: These dogmatic words and terms are indispensable because they have stored within them the spiritual knowledge of a long history of faith. But as such receptacles they can be used only in the theological laboratory. They are intended only for internal, official use. And within this context they serve as convenient abbreviations, stenographic means of making oneself understood.

This is precisely the reason why they are false when they appear unchanged in the mouth of the witness. They become false not only because the ordinary person cannot understand them at all or because he misunderstands them (for example, in a moralistic sense), but also because in the mouth of the witness they must show that he himself has worked through and experienced the truths which are stored up in them. For, after all, the witness not only confesses and declares his *message*, he also confesses and declares his *encounter* with the message. Consequently, he also speaks of himself, simply because of the fact that he stands up for the truth he is witnessing. But he can do this only if he communicates to his hearers the fact that he himself has experienced this truth.

You certainly must not think that this means he must constantly be displaying his spiritual autobiography to his hearers. True, there are such unappetizing self-revealers and spiritual autobiographers. But they are examples of a degenerated witness which do not let us forget that all legitimate testimony must also set forth the witness himself, and show that he stands back of what he says. This, as we have pointed out, is the only reason why the question of the credibility of the witness is so important. This is why it is just as important as the question of the credibility of the message, the testimony itself.

But if this is the way things are, then the theological vocabulary becomes even more questionable whenever it is taken out of the laboratory and placed unchanged in the mouth of the witness. That is to say, one can juggle with these terms in the laboratory. One can compare the way in which they are used, for example, by Irenaeus, Augustine, Luther, and Schleiermacher. In this juggling (intentionally expressing it in this somewhat brash way) one does not always have to keep revealing how one stands with regard to the truths which are contained in these abbreviations. In theological work one is a little removed from the truths, just as a doctor who is making a blood test, an electrocardiogram, or an X-ray examination may for the moment abandon his primary commitment as a "physician" and not be thinking at every moment that here he is dealing with the fate of a living person and that he must actually maintain an *existential* attitude toward what comes out in the laboratory.

But even though this laboratory use of theological terms is legitimate, it all becomes strange and inappropriate when it appears undigested and untranslated in the pulpit. Then just because the witness is always confessing himself along with his message, it now appears, when the traditional terms are blithely and doctrinally correctly strung together, as if the witness has the same close existential relationship to all of them, as if he had experienced all of them in his own life. But this is a lie, it is *false* witness. Can a man in every hour of his life confess as "his" truths all the truths of the Apostles' Creed? Good heavens, who can keep saying in every moment "I believe in the Holy Ghost"? Are not these truths far too steep and towering simply to be on call and be blithely confessed at any moment?

But are we not witnessing and preaching about our own real

relationship when we take all this, simply because it is all there, ready-packed and completely linked together in the catechisms, and hand it out to the people, giving the impression that all this is present in the pastor, that he is a warehouse of all the truths which are our one hope in life and in death? Is not this an existential lie? May not this be like handing out rubber checks?

The Fear of Saying Too Little

An art student once characterized the listener's situation that results from this existential lie. He said, "Why are you always setting forth your multitude of truths and blinding us as with a thousand-watt lamp? We are moles who have just crawled out of the ground and we can stand the light only of a small candle, we can bear only a very small truth. But you descend upon us with the floodlight of all the truths of the centuries. You serve up everything at once. Please, just one candle, one single candle!"

This young man was honest enough to be afraid of having to believe too much all at once; for he knew he could not digest it. And therefore it would have been a lie if he had persuaded himself that now all of this was *his* truth, truths which he believed. But is not the manipulator of Christian words up there in the pulpit making the same untruthful mistake? Everything he says may be true. But as witness it is untrue. It is far worse, it is an abomination before God, to believe (or to imagine one believes) too much rather than too little. Only twice did Jesus speak of a person's having great faith and give it great respect. But in both cases these persons believed very little quantitatively speaking; nevertheless, what they did believe was genuine and genuinely experienced.

But if we take this seriously, where does it take us? Would not this mean that we may preach only fragments of the Christian truths, that we can speak only of what has become a certainty in our own life and experience and possibly only in the moment we utter it?

To draw this conclusion is so absurd that we know we are on the wrong track. The minister cannot say: I still do not know what I believe about Easter; therefore I shall stop with my Good Friday sermon. I do not know what to do with Christmas, but if need be I can preach an Advent sermon on expectant man. No, he is bound to the whole truth; and this *Christian* truth is likewise indivisible.

There will, however, be differentiations in his preaching which will make it evident whether he is talking about a truth which he has experienced or which is still beyond him. Therefore he must be able to confess that he is helpless at certain points, just as Luther, for example, never wearied of admitting about certain dark passages of Scripture. Luther then did not suppress these passages or exclude them from the canon, but rather advised the preacher to take off his hat and pass them by—but in any case to show his reverence for them! Such a reverent gesture indicates that we recognize that the truth of God is always greater than our faith and that the spiritual knowledge of the church is greater than our spiritual experience. Even when I bear witness to that which I must pass by in reverence or that which hitherto has passed me by and has not yet spoken to me, I can still bear a real witness. But then it will have a different sound. The lie begins only when everything sounds equally and uniformly certain. Not only the witness must have his own tone; every one of his testimonies must have its own tone. Where it supports the temple of genuineness it is richly instrumented.

I once heard of a preacher who practiced this in a very drastic way. He had to bury the mother of three small children. She had been killed in a traffic accident. The meaninglessness of the accident, the utter misery of the young husband and the young children, so overwhelmed him that he had to confess: "I know the words of Holy Scripture which are appropriate for such an hour of desolation and trial as this, but I cannot utter them here. I myself am far too helpless and overcome with pain. Even those devout words stick in my throat. I will speak them to you later. There is only one thing I can do now: Let us pray together the Lord's Prayer."

This young preacher was honest. He differentiated between truths which were at his disposal and others which at this moment were beyond his reach. In his despair he retreated to the innermost line of defense in his faith—to the prayer of the Lord. But look what happened: the Holy Spirit entered in and took his place and testified vicariously for him who could find nothing to say. The miracle happened—everyone there went away comforted. They heard what was absolutely genuine and there was no false note in what was said. By not uttering the words of comfort ("My thoughts are not your thoughts . . .") the preacher did not deny the cause which had been committed to him and he did not disown the Lord who had given him that commission. Rather he acknowledged and confessed all this by taking refuge in the last corner of his faith, the Lord's Prayer.

That is why we should rather say too little than too much. Even spiritually we dare not "talk too big." Above all we must make differentiations and indicate which truths we are still waiting to experience. Then we can also confess and extol them as expected truths. And when we do this we are proclaiming that the truth of the Holy Scriptures and of the church is greater than our faith. Then we are testifying that we do not have faith in our own faith (because it is far too paltry and because it is what it is—an expectant faith). But woe to him who acts as if he already "saw" all things, as if everything were equally clear to him, as if he were looking without blinking into the thousand-watt lamp of the whole truth.

But a differentiation between what I know for sure and what is still not a part of my experience is important, not only for reasons of simple honesty, but also from the point of view of method. Then it is a matter of intellectual order and clarity. Nobody can say everything at one time without exposing himself to the danger of saying nothing. Therefore the sermon, which should be an intellectual organism, must have a central point; each individual sermon must have an organizing center that grows out of the text. Like any other portrait, the portrait of the gospel requires the art of omission, or at least a distinction between what is to be sketched and what is to be drawn fully. It was, of all people, Aloys Henhöfer (b. 1789), the solid revival preacher who certainly could not be accused of curtailing the gospel, who said concerning his sermons in the little village of Spöck in Baden that he did not want to preach rabbit sermons but stag sermons. "A hunter who is out to shoot the stag lets the rabbits go; otherwise he will drive away the stag."[13] So in hunting and in preaching one must know what one is after, and then one must concentrate on that. Therefore one cannot say everything in every sermon. But the conventional dogmatic terms contain "everything." That is why they are so dangerous.

All honor to the so-called "whole" gospel! We certainly are not pleading for any reduction—to moral truths, for example. But then what do we mean by "uncurtailed" and "whole"? Does this mean that one must spell out everything in every sermon? Is everything spelled out in every New Testament pericope? Did not every dialogue of Jesus likewise have its central point? The fact is that when I express one thing *wholly* (for example, the message of the forgiveness of sins) I have thereby implicitly expressed everything else: the message of Christ's death on the cross, the resurrection, indeed, even the doctrines of creation and eschatology. All praise to the courage to be implicit! For the Christian truths are like microcosms in which the whole cosmos is portrayed. I therefore do not speak the truth in the form of quantitative expatiation upon all truths. I rather speak the truth by choosing one of its microcosms and then searching it and penetrating to its core. This is not only the proper way to approach the thing itself but is also suited to the hearers' capacity of comprehension.

Two Theologians in Dialogue

He who attempts to say everything not only says nothing but is also in danger of proceeding from a wrong conception of justification. When a man attempts to say everything is he not proceeding on the assumption that he has to do and proclaim everything himself? Is he not trying to pacify his conscience (which is constraining him to bear faithful witness) by wanting to demonstrate that he has really said "everything" and left out nothing? Does not this cause him quickly to throw in another subordinate clause in order to be sure he has gotten it in and said it (though nobody in this world could ever find it in this obscure corner or even judge its importance).

He who attempts to bring the whole schema of Trinity, creation, redemption, and eschatology into his sermon cannot help but produce a pale and diluted effect.

I am reminded here of a conversation I heard take place between two fairly well-known professors of theology. They were complaining about the fact that most sermons are not vivid and graphic, that they are colorless and superficial. It will be best perhaps to reproduce the conversation briefly.

PROFESSOR X (to his colleague Y): This, of course, is not true of you. You have the gift of vividness and anecdote, your speech has light and shadow, a pictorial quality. But I, on the other hand, am a rather miserable preacher. My students complain that I stand in the pulpit like a codfish, racing on from sentence to sentence without any articulation, without raising or lowering my voice, never changing in stress or emphasis. People fall asleep listening to me. I simply cannot speak in an interesting way.

PROFESSOR Y: I do not believe that this is related primarily to a man's rhetorical gift. On the contrary, I think that this lack of interest and color is deeply connected with the nature of your theology.

PROFESSOR X: In what way?

PROFESSOR Y: Well, not long ago you asked what I taught about the angels. You were shocked when I answered, "Nothing at all!" So far I have said nothing about it because I still have no real relationship or experience with this truth.

PROFESSOR X: As a matter of fact, I was rather astonished. After all, as a professor of theology a man must be able to say something about it. But I do not understand what that has to do with interesting preaching.

PROFESSOR Y: A great deal! Look, you represent a type of theological thinking which is much interested in the formal structure of the dogmatic system. It *does* have this structure, and I admit that it can give one a lot of intellectual pleasure to see how one dogmatic locus gears into the other and how the doctrine of creation is logically connected with the Last Judgment. One who delights in architectonic symmetry can perhaps enjoy the orthodox system with a real *amor theologiae intellectualis*.

PROFESSOR X: Yes—and? Is it not our job as teachers of theology to bring out this systematic structure? Don't you do the same thing?

PROFESSOR Y: Yes, naturally, and very vigorously too. But perhaps I do it somewhat differently from you.

PROFESSOR X: That is clear. We certainly do not have the same theology. And we have also been stamped by quite different schools and in our work we concentrate on quite different areas.

PROFESSOR Y: Naturally. But that is not at all what I meant when I said that I had a different attitude from yours toward the structure of the theological system.

PROFESSOR X: What did you mean?

PROFESSOR Y: Our old friendship permits me to speak quite frankly. You remind me of a general reviewing all the theological truths. You look each one in the face (and perhaps each individual theological truth into whose eyes you look feels that you have penetrated to the depths of its soul). But as you review these truths you are at an equal distance from all of them. After all, the general dare not walk along the line in a zigzag path, sometimes one yard and sometimes two yards away. That's how the flatness and monotony (even in the tone of your voice!) gets into your theology and even more into your preaching.

PROFESSOR X: And you think it is otherwise with you?

PROFESSOR Y: Yes, that's what I believe, though I do not assert that it is a matter of merit. You saw the difference in the question of the angels. For you this truth about the angels stands alongside of other truths (such as Christ's death on the cross) in the line which you are reviewing. And, as we said, you are equally near to all of these truths. I, on the other hand, distinguish between what has really been borne in upon me, what has come close to me, and other areas of truth which are still remote from me, which are as it were still beyond me. And in my lectures and even more in the pulpit I let my hearers know this.

PROFESSOR X: And what has that to do with the vividness of a man's language?

PROFESSOR Y: That seems to me to be very easy to understand. Vividness is a matter of perspective. Perspective means that what I see and what I portray for others is related to the observer's standpoint and that it always communicates my relationship to things too. And this is where I think there are two differences between us. You have no "perspective" in your theology; it is all flat. And that means, first, that there is no distinction between what is nearer and what is more remote, between what is primary and what is secondary, and so there is also no focal point; and second, you do not reveal your own relationship or attitude to these things, that is, you do not emerge as a perspective center. And the result is that there is no vividness.

PROFESSOR X: That's an argument that rather bewilders me. You mean to say that vivid preaching has no connection with a man's intellectual consititution and a definite gift of imagination but that it is rather dependent upon one's thought structure and one's relationship to truth.

PROFESSOR Y: I do not believe that we can divide the two as precisely as that. Certainly our intellectual constitution does contribute to the formation of our theology. And yet we dare not imagine that differences in theologies are due *only* to differing relationships to the question of truth. Do you think that Luther and Calvin (say in their doctrine of law and gospel) arrived at different decisions with regard to the truth *only* because of theological reasons? Just look at the "pyknic" Luther and this "asthenoleptosomatic" Calvin! It would be ridiculous if this did not have some influence on their theology. But please do not interpret this to mean that I want to pander to a relativism which would make theology dependent on constitutional and possible chthonic-telluric factors.

PROFESSOR X: No, I would not accuse you of drawing that conclusion. On the contrary, on this point we are in complete agreement. I too believe that in theology not everything is only theology but that we must also take into account other contributing factors from other areas in order to understand a theology. There are nontheological factors in theology; this is the human thing about it. And therefore we can never simply take over a theology, for then we take over not only the theology itself but also the man who propounded it.

PROFESSOR Y: I'm glad that we see eye to eye on that point. Incidentally, the mention of Luther and Calvin suggests to me the idea that it is possible with their help to illustrate very nicely the problem of vivid preaching.

PROFESSOR Y: You are—if you will pardon me—constitutionally a Calvinist and I a Lutheran.

PROFESSOR X: Help!

PROFESSOR Y: Now, Luther in his thinking distinguished between this nearness and remoteness which we have been talking about. The problem of justification was very close to him, whereas eschatology was certainly much further away. And also among the books of the Bible there were some which were very close to him and others which he did not understand and did not like. In the Book of Esther there is too much "Judaizing" for him, the Epistle of James was for him a "straw" epistle, the Revelation of John was not Christocentric enough. But, mind you, he swallowed the Epistle to the Romans whole. Calvin, however, walked down the line reviewing the books of the Bible and the dogmas (just as you do!) and was equally close to all of them. That made Luther vivid and Calvin far more colorless (which is, of course, no reflection upon the profundity of what he said).

PROFESSOR X: Well, even if it is only a play on ideas, I must admit that it is interesting. In any case one must think about it. And I would not venture to deny that it is worthwhile thinking about the question of what our personal relationship and attitude is toward the individual truths. To be sure, it is always a fruitful thing for people like us to find a way of not regarding one's own peculiarities, faults, and virtues in the pulpit and the lecture room as being based primarily upon psychological and constitutional factors, but rather to be led to ask whether they may not be rooted deep in our "theological existence" and therefore be connected with the way in which we theologize and relate ourselves to the truth.

So much for this conversation which I have reproduced from memory and rounded off a bit editorially.

Why is it that the statements of the Ecumenical Council and so many other ecclesiastical statements are so colorless? Why do they not "hit home"? Because they want to say *too much*, because they want to speak too *guardedly*, with too many qualifications, and therefore never summon up the courage to make a strong point. The more editorial cooks there are stirring the broth, the more any relationship to the truth of a concrete existence is lost and thus the greater is the loss of perspective and therefore of vividness. In order to be vivid, however, one must have the courage to make one central point and therefore to be content to be incomplete. We must let the rabbits go today—not because they are less important than the stag, but because *today* we are hunting stags.

As we said, it can be a sign of unbelief if we try to justify ourselves by everything and trust that by this slavish, legalistic faithfulness we have done our duty to the truth. Thus we overload the sermon with human work. For completeness too is human work.

Quite apart from this false doctrine of justification with the disastrous paralyzing effect it has upon the listeners, there is this too that should be remembered. The preacher is permitted to trust that it is not only today that he will be standing in the pulpit, but that he will go on preaching and in this way the main points will be made more and more complete. Besides, he is only *one* voice in the symphony of the church's preaching. He should not imagine that with his one poor voice he is the whole concert—and even the whole concert today and in this hour. The church of Jesus Christ will go on preaching until the Last Day and the gates of hell will not prevail against it. Therefore we should not try to crowd all eternity into one sermon. Only the devil's time is short;[14] and only the faithless are worried that time may be in his hands and not in the hands of God.[15] The man who wants to say everything in one sermon will also be a promoter in other respects, a man who will speed up the ecclesiastical machinery to a hectic tempo. Here again he imagines that eternity depends upon how he fills up time. Here give me Luther who knew how to stop and trust God like a child, the man who could say: While I sit here drinking my pot of Wittenberg beer, the gospel runs its course. (It runs on by itself, even when I am not in the pulpit. In other words, there is Another with us on the field.)

A *Brief Look in the Sermon Laboratory*

I know what the theological experts will say about my putting such stress upon the idea of having a central point in the sermon. They will say that I am leading people away from the real interpretation of the text and seducing them into thematic or topical preaching. Even those who do not immediately understand what this technical discussion is all about may be interested in the problems it involves, for these have their appeal for anybody who has a taste for questions of method.

Briefly stated, the question is this. Ever since Karl Barth and his theology gave new stimulus to preaching there has been a controversy that revolves around the words "textual sermon" and "thematic sermon."[16] What is meant by a textual sermon is a meditative presentation in which one goes through the text, following its train of thought, considering and taking seriously every word in it, and thus as far as possible exploring and exhausting the whole of it. It is especially the Barthian school which has committed itself in theory and practice to this method of preaching, and not without good reasons. For it had sufficient cause to detest and regard as a misuse of the holy texts the then prevailing thematic sermon, which was popular in the nineteenth century and which liberal theology had made the magna carta of homiletics. The more preachers became estranged from the Bible and the more they courted the favor of the spirit of the times, the more the sermon became a lecture on some theme, such as "Man and Culture," "The Ethical Problem of the Sermon on the Mount," "The Nature of Love." (To this day such themes can be seen on the bulletin boards of Unitarian churches in America.) Naturally, ancient custom required that the preacher should read a Scripture text from the pulpit and even that it should constitute the ostensible basis of the sermon. But often it was difficult to bring the theme and the text into agreement; the one said more or less than the other, and often the purpose of the theme and the text was widely disparate. But since the heart of the preacher was set on his theme, on which he proposed to prepare a sonorous essay, the text was degraded to the level of a mere motto or even a mere refrain. The text was repeatedly quoted as an illustration or to underscore and corroborate what was said; but it was understood that its meaning, that is, its message, could not be taken very literally. It was something like the sound-track music in modern films; it constitutes a background noise which has an independent purpose of its own. Therefore the less it obtrudes itself and the more it is content to make a quiet appeal to the unconscious mind, the better it is. Over against this, Gottfried Menken, who was averse to the whole cult of the Zeitgeist, said shortly before 1800: "In my opinion Satan dealt a major blow to the kingdom of God when he succeeded in dislodging the old biblical-analytical method [i.e., textual preaching] and introducing the synthetic method [i.e., thematic preaching]. When preachers began to use the Word of God as a book of aphorisms and used the text as nothing more than a motto and, instead of expounding a word of God for the people, talked about some general theme floating in the air, all the usefulness of preaching was done for."[17]

Certainly this states a genuine alternative and we need not add anything to it—unless it be the question of what we should do with it in practice and the question whether my insistence upon having a main point is not rather uncomfortably close to thematic preaching.

I believe that this is not so; for it all depends upon *what* the theme is, whether it be one that the preacher takes from life and then simply hangs his text upon it, misusing it as a motto, or whether he takes the theme from the text itself and with its aid formulates the main point of this text. These are obviously two very different breeds of themes and they can hardly be compared with each other. And I choose this latter textual-thematic kind of preaching, and for three different reasons.

First, in this way one remains within the text and allows it to be an end in itself. One discovers in it a center and a periphery and one illuminates it on the basis of its main ideas.

Second, this way of determining the theme not only helps to keep the sermon true to the text but also helps the preacher to achieve order and clarity. If he merely proceeds word by word in the style of a homily, making his comments as he goes along, the unifying bond may easily slip away from him. Then ordinary people, with no great capacity for organizing the thoughts that are presented, are confronted with a chaotic mess of ideas. And finally the listener does not know what comes first and what comes next. Anyone who values intellectual clarity suffers the pangs of hell listening to it and keeps groaning: "There again he took that curve too fast or too short. How did he suddenly get to this point? Angels must have borne him there! Anyhow I can't find any connection! There he should have lingered for a moment and not left it with a subordinate clause. Has the man confused the brake with the accelerator?"

Great masters can handle this difficult method with great skill. I would think that Karl Barth himself (unlike many of his small-bore disciples) has shown what an expert can do with this demanding method. The study of the text and theme together, however, makes it easier to gain clarity and order, easier to arrive at an outline which makes the whole sermon transparent. In any case, beginners can handle it more easily.

Third, this method is also more helpful to the hearer. He retains it better and can more readily pass it on to others. I still remember the outline of a New Year's Day sermon which the pastor of my old home town congregation contrived:

"We look
  1. gratefully backward
  2. joyfully forward
  3. believingly upward."

That I could tell to my grandmother when she asked me what the sermon was about. Naturally, it was a bit old-fashioned, and I am not advising anyone to repeat this outline literally. It was also too close to the usual stereotype of a New Year's Day sermon. With a bit of humor, however, you will understand what I am driving at.

But the thematic sermon is helpful most of all to hearers who are interested in a question and perhaps have no desire to listen to any biblical exposition whatsoever.

This will be true especially of those who are on the fringes or outside of the church. They may sit up and take notice when they find that the theme announced is "The Meaning of Life" and perhaps they will be much surprised to hear a sermon on the Rich Young Ruler subsumed under this theme. They may also have to recognize that some unexpected problems are dealt with in the Bible.

All this has been only a brief look into the homiletical laboratory—that is to say, the preacher's study; we have shared in his cogitations on the question: "How shall I tell it to my child?"

But the mistakes that can be made here are not merely homiletical peccadillos. The fundamental problem with which we started, the problem of honesty in our spiritual existence and its expression in speech, leads us into far more frightening and darker depths. And I should like now to speak of this fundamental crisis from another angle.

Abstract Man—the Wrong Man to Address

The real crisis of preaching under which we are suffering and which fills us with concern whether we have "death in the pot" is not one that has to do with form or is attributable to mistakes in form. We indicated what the spiritual root of it is when we raised the question whether the preacher himself lives in the house of his preaching, whether he is a credible, convincing witness. Now I should like to say something about the *theological* root of this crisis. For this it does have! All great crises of preaching have always come out of a false theology. But how can I make such a general, wholesale judgment and say that our theology is false?

After all, what *is* our theology? Are we not confronted today with a great variety of current theologies, all of which are characterized by more or less famous names? And *I* should be so bold as to say in this wholesale and obviously unjust and generalizing way: Our theology is false (except probably my own!)?

Perhaps it would be better to express it more precisely and say: Something is false in almost all of our theologies. What then?

Using a term which is familiar to the professionals who have studied the history of doctrine, I should say that our theologies are suffering from a modern variant of *Docetism*. Naturally, I must explain this.[18]

Originally—in ancient church history—the term "Docetism" was used to denote a heretical variant of Christology. The heresy consisted in the fact that the Docetists conceded to Christ only a phantom corporeality and thus did not wish, as Luther would say, to "draw him too deeply into the flesh." In his essence he was the "Son of God." And it seemed hardly in keeping with the divine attributes which went along with this—indeed, it seemed actually downright contradictory and absurd—to ascribe to him at the same time the marks of human existence, such as limitedness, finitude, culpability, and the ability to suffer. Even the category of creatureliness appeared to be improper with respect to Christ. He was not "created" like other creatures, but was rather "begotten of the Father" (though this differentiation need not be labeled Docetism). The experts know the controversies in the history of dogma to which I am referring. It is sufficient here to state that Docetism denied the humanity of Christ (at any rate the full humanity which is subject to the pressure of history) in order not to endanger his divine status and therefore his ability to be a redeemer. The result was the conception of a more or less spectral heavenly being, who lacked any real solidarity with human existence. Modern liberal theology constitutes a curious antithesis to this position in so far as it reverses the ancient heresy as it were and sees in Christ only an ultimate culmination of humanity, a *homo religiosissimus*, to whom divine attributes are at most symbolically ascribed.

This ancient-church Docetism appears today in a modified, but equally disastrous way, except that it crops up at a different place. It has, so to speak, slipped over from Christology into anthropology. Now we sepak of *man* in an abstract, general way, as if he had only a phantom body.

Gerhard Ebeling has rightly pointed out that "the concept 'reality'—ironically enough!—is one of the most abstract things one can imagine."[19] The statement we often hear made with some emotion from the pulpit that "God is not an idea but a reality," is an intellectual fraud because here one reduces God to an abstraction while seeming to assert just the opposite.

Exactly the same thing applies to the way in which we speak of "man," who does not exist at all as this nominalistic collective concept. And yet this collective term is common parlance in the pulpit as well as in the theological lecture hall. So the real, individual man who sits beneath the pulpit or the lectern feels quite untouched whenever this phantom being is mentioned. He is incapable of performing the task here imposed upon him of subsuming himself as an individual case under this general category.

Stated more precisely, what then does the Docetic misunderstanding of man mean?

It consists in removing man from the history that pervades him and swallows him up, in isolating him from his "world." One need only read an excerpt from Bultmann's essay, "The Understanding of Man and the World in the New Testament and in the Greek World," to catch what I mean: "The New Testament sees the monstrous power of this sphere—the 'world'—it sees that the 'world' with its pleasures and cares divests man of genuine care about himself, distracting him from the search for God and the transcendent, which fixes the bounds of this world. It sees that men who are in the grip of the world trouble themselves and worry about things which are transient; and thus it sees the 'world' as passing away, and characterized by death. Man, then, is indeed in the grip of the world and, so to speak, embedded in it—but for his ruin, not for his salvation."[20]

There is no doubt that all this is to be found in the New Testament, but obviously it is only *one* side of the coin. Does it not also bear witness to the freedom of man in this his world? Is not the world here revealed to him as the place where God desires to meet him in His works as well as in the neighbor? Is it not the realm of his gifts and responsibilities—a realm which is opened up for him by reason of his being called out of it and sent back into it? Is not the world the sphere which God so loved that he "sent his only begotten Son"? Dare one, therefore, really think of the world only as the power which holds man in its grip?

If one nevertheless *insists* upon thinking of it in this way, then it is no wonder that the only way to be able to see the real man is to isolate him from this alien power 'the world," that the only way he can be seen in his actual being is to strip off this heteronomous element. But if we do this, he becomes a worldless specter, an abstraction with a phantom body. For "this aeon" is not an accidental of his being which can be subtracted without danger of loss of substance; rather this world belongs to his very nature and being. The structure of this world, with its inhibitory laws, its autonomous trends, and its pitiless harshness, is only a macrocosmic likeness of his heart. And conversely, the human heart is only the microcosmic expression of this his world. "All man's Babylons strive but to impart / The grandeurs of his Babylonian heart" (Francis Thompson).[21] "Man" is man *in* his world and not man *apart* from his world. And if, as Bultmann says, the world is a chain that binds him, then this chain would be precisely the mark of his existence between the Fall and the Last Judgment and then this nature of his existence could not be described without applying to it this existential attribute of the chain. But I submit that if one thus interprets the world only as a chain, the temptation is all too great to set forth man "in himself" ("*an sich*"), and this means describing him *without* the chain. Then "man" is this man in his state of being unchained. This is why the listener, the real man who is gripped and squeezed by his world and is really enchained by it, does not recognize himself in that strange, denatured, and abstract double of himself.

This Docetism in the sphere of humanity undoubtedly infil-
trated into theology by way of existentialism. The very name
Bultmann suggests this association. Here "the external world . . .
confronts man from the very outset as something which is hostile
and restrictive of his free movement."[22] The world appears as
something by which human existence is essentially hampered and
confined, something which—as Sartre significantly says—"fixates"
him. In Heidegger "the world dwindles into the two ways of being,
the ready-to-hand (*Zuhandenen*) and the present-at-hand (*Vor-
handenen*), to the realm of the technically useful, and from there,
since it is a world which is regarded as a deficient *modus* (!), to
naked reality stripped of all meaning. There are no spheres of
reality which are filled with their own meaning, whether they be
the organic life of the animals and plants or the sphere of human
culture in the sense of its having any value. And in a corresponding way, for Jaspers the whole orientation of the world is directed
toward making external provision for existence. Before the absolute splendor of authentic existence the whole world sinks to the
level of a meaningless background."[23] It is undoubtedly this *trend*
toward the "absolute splendor of authentic existence" which allows Docetism to get into anthropology. This is what causes us
to speak of "man" and to mean by this the supposedly "real" who
is set apart from his world and freed from its fixation.

We can hardly overestimate the extent to which this conception
(which, naturally, is not confined to existentialism but ranges far
beyond it temporally and spatially) has corrupted our theology
and our preaching. This is the root of what has been called its
abstractness, its colorlessness, and its debility. And the rank
growths which it had proliferated are not made any less active and
destructively rampant by the fact that the root of it has gone
largely unrecognized. People think in all innocence that because
one speaks about man one is close to men, and because one talks
about reality one is realistic. How strange then (but is it really so

strange?) that hardly anybody feels that he has been addressed
and touched and that obviously it is altogether different shoes
which are pinching the children of this world.

The Man Who Does Not Exist

I am searching for an example which will show how this Docetism
works itself out in preaching. Quite generally it may be presumed
that a sermon so structured will be definitely individualistic. For,
after all, it emphasizes man "as such," man isolated from the
world. This becomes apparent, for example, when we see the way
in which this kind of preacher deals with the commandment to
love one's neighbor and one's enemy.

This preacher will presumably talk quite simply about "two
men" who confront each other as neighbors or as enemies. And
here already the questions begin: Do these "two men" exist at all?
What is their sex, their age, their vocation, their definite social and
geographical situation? Does it make no difference whether they
confront each other as landlords or as renters, business competi-
tors, or as persons who are attracted to each other by erotic
feeling? What becomes of two "neighbors" who are married and
have drifted apart in the realm of eros? Does the commandment
"Love your neighbor" mean that one can simply ignore the special
forms which the separative element (the opposite of love) takes?
Does it mean that agape can take the place of eros? But what if
the combination of eros and agape continues to function? Is Christian agape then something that is lived on a totally *different* level,
or does it include eros within itself? And then what is the nature of
this combination of eros and agape?[24]

Question upon question! Obviously, therefore, this commandment is not simply a matter of "two men" who are to love each
other, but rather of two men "in situation," in a *definite* situation,
to whom this challenge applies and whose situation is also affected
by the commandment of love. If they have to be "enjoined" to

love, this means that these two men are not *of themselves* insisting upon this love but that something threatens to get between them and prevent the love which is required of them.

But what is this? Is it really only self-love, which overlooks or crowds out the other person? What does self-love mean? I am afraid that here again we have an individualistic term, which makes that which separates me from my neighbor Docetic and unreal. For even my self-love is not a purely internal emotion, but is always connected with my being-in-the-world, and therefore with my situation. There is an *erotic* self-love that desires to be satisfied. There is an *economic* self-love that would like to assert itself by its accomplishments. There is a *political* self-love that presses toward collective self-assertion, which ever since the days of Machiavelli has been called *sacro egoismo* and thus a legitimate self-love. But if this is the case, if self-love is not only produced by my wicked heart, but is connected with certain structures of my being-in-the-world, then I obviously cannot simply dismiss it or label it forthwith as something that must be eliminated. But then in no case can I speak of self-love in an abstract, Docetic way and again turn it into an abstract collective word. Then I must rather differentiate between the various forms of self-love. And here again we must look for an illustration.[25]

It may perhaps be possible for me to interpret the commandment of neighborly love vividly and interestingly in this individualistic, Docetic sense. The Docetists, after all, can be imaginative and attractive speakers. Thus, for example, the preacher can speak in very lively fashion of the fact that I should read to that old person who lives in my neighborhood, that I should say a kind word to my depressed neighbor, that I should make arrangements with my bank for continuing contributions for the starving children of India. The Docetic preacher may have many colors on his palette and nobody need fall asleep listening to him. And I certainly do not deny that they are bright and genuine colors. And yet after the service a young businessman comes to see the preacher in his sacristy and says to him: "Everything you said was fine and good. But unfortunately my own situation never entered the picture." The preacher replies with some surprise: "How is that?" And the businessman says: "Well, you don't really have to tell me that stuff about reading to an old person and saying a good word to a depressed friend. I am so good-natured and philanthropic by nature that I do this of my own accord. Anybody who is good-hearted cannot do otherwise. Even some of my non-Christian friends do the same thing. But if I want to live quite consciously as a *Christian*, there are some altogether different questions that trouble me, for example, this one. I am a businessman who has to meet competition. And God knows it's stiff. My chief competitor is not far away from me; in fact, he lives on the same street I do. I know him and his family very well. So I have to 'get along' with him in many ways. But this is where my question comes in: *How* shall I love my competitor? I am a better businessman than he is, I know the ropes better than he does. I also have more capital and therefore I can maneuver more freely. I have a 'nose' for market developments. My advantage is so great that as my business prospers his declines. Now, quite concretely, what does it mean for me that I should love him?

"Naturally it cannot mean that I should merely cherish certain sentimental feelings toward him and that I should merely put myself in his situation (though this too is demanded). But then, what does it mean? Does 'loving' here mean that I should buy at higher prices, offer inferior products, and artificially cut down my volume of business? In other words, am I no longer to fight the battle of competition according to its own laws or must I soften these rules philanthropically and therefore act in an unbusinesslike way? As a Christian does this mean that I must operate only at half steam? Must I be prepared possibly to go on the rocks even economically for the sake of love? But if I do this, cease to be competitive, and perhaps have to close my business, what will happen to my employees, to whom I am *also* obligated to be a neighbor?

"Don't you see? This is where my problem lies. As you said in your sermon, 'Love means to be there for others.' I agree with that. But in what *way* can I be there for him? As a 'self' I am Businessman X, I am in a very definite economic and business situation. Does all this belong to my 'self'? Or are these economic and situational factors something for which I am not responsible; are they factors that simply exert force upon me from the outside and therefore are they in a specific way a 'not-self,' a *heteros nomos?* (Here we are letting this businessman talk as if he had taken a couple of semesters of theology or sociology!) Am I or am I not what operates along *with* me and *through* me?

"Here I am perhaps different from the man in the New Testament who asked Jesus, 'Who is my neighbor?'[26] I think I know the answer to that because I have read and perhaps understand at least a little the parable of the Good Samaritan. What I would like to ask is: Who am *I*, who is to be a neighbor to my neighbor? Am I only the individual who can be isolated from his vocation and his situation in the world? Or in my capacity as a neighbor do I still remain a businessman (or, for that matter, a party politician)? But then what does this love of my neighbor which God demands of me look like?"

We can present another variation of this question of the man who listened to the sermon: What allows me to be "historical" and *through what* am I "in encounter," through what am I in "being-toward-the-thou"? Obviously I am "historical" and "in encounter" only by way of the structures of history, through the media of transsubjective data. As Jaspers says, I am always "in situation." To be "in situation," however, can mean only that I stand in vocational, economic, political, erotic, and other relationships to others.

But then we are immediately faced with the next question of

how these structures are to be interpreted theologically. I have two alternatives. The first is to interpret these structures as that which I myself am *not*, as that into which I have been "thrown." Then I can effect this separation of these other relationships from myself by regarding my situation in the world as given in creation. God simply made the world as it is. Then, as Kant says, I stand, as it were, *over against* the "inherited structures (*Anlagen*) of man and his world. Then I am not responsible for them. They are simply given, simply my lot. But I can also effect this separation from myself by saying: This is simply the fallen world into which I have been *thrown*. And here too it is regarded as a suprapersonal fate for which I have no responsibility.

The other alternative is for me to admit that the world so structured is "my" world and that therefore it is, as we said above, the macrocosmic reflection of my heart. Then I must say to this my world: *Tat tvam asi*—this I am. Then the competitive struggle, which confronts me as a suprapersonal power, is only the expression of that which determines the structure of my heart as it structures the world.

But then I can no longer say: *Here* am "I," who desires the good, and *there* is the evil world, which compels me to assume such questionable attitudes. Then I must rather regard myself as the subject of that which the evil world seems to compel me to do. Then we shall be dealing with an indivisible reality. Then the "I" can no longer be Docetically isolated and separated from that reality.

It would seem that the Sermon on the Mount chooses this latter alternative. For it is not content—as is Kant's ethics—to make demands of me on the basis of given "inherited structures" and therefore in the framework of situations which are regarded as fateful, but rather above and beyond all the given facts, even beyond the libido[27] and actual laws of this aeon.[28] It places me and my whole world under its radical demands and therefore looks upon me and my world as an indivisible reality. This goes so far that the Sermon on the Mount has actually been called "other-worldly" because it simply disregards the structure of this world. And the fact is that it *does*. But in doing so its purpose is not to be other-worldly, but rather to show that this our world is alien to the kingdom of God, that it no longer reflects complete conformity with God and that even structurally it has been implicated in the Fall of man. The Sermon on the Mount lays its demands upon us as if we were still in the original state and as if the kingdom of God has already come. Therefore it gives offense everywhere—to our subjectivity and also to the structure of the world.

But then *everything* we do is in need of forgiveness, even that which we do in the name of the order and structure of the world. And the devout soldier, who is defending his country and knows that this is not contrary to the will of God, will sometimes think of the fact that the war, in which he is being obedient and therefore seeking to comply with the will of God, is the expression of a world structure which God did *not* will. And when he prays the Lord's Prayer and says, "Forgive us our trespasses," he will not only think of what he has done wrong as an individual, but this petition will also relate to what he must now do in the context of this world structure.[29]

If it is true that we must thus see man *together* with his world and that he must by no means be isolated from it, then this has very great significance not only for theological ethics but also for the whole realm of theological anthropology. Then it involves, for example, the demand that we rethink the doctrine of sin and the doctrine of the orders: the doctrine of *sin* in so far as sin then attaches not only to the status of the individual but also to the supraindividual status of the world, and since from this point of view we get a wholly new view of the transsubjective aspects of the doctrine of original sin; and the doctrine of the *orders* in so far as they represent the structural forms of this aeon, which as such can never be pure orders of creation but are at the same time objectifications of human sin and therefore have a shadow cast upon them. New light also falls upon *eschatology:* the world which is so structured cannot of itself produce the realization of the pure will of God. Therefore the kingdom of God is not a state which could develop evolutionally out of this world. Therefore it is rather the power which comes to us from the other side of the boundary of this world. Therefore its coming also means the downfall of the world. Therefore we pray, not "Thy kingdom emerge," but rather "Thy kingdom come"!

The businessman we quoted above, under the pressure of his existential situation, saw the problem very clearly when he asked whether the autonomy of competition, which is obviously operative as a structural form of this aeon, somehow belongs to him (so that he must be responsible for it and everything he does within its framework) or whether it is only a transsubjective law to which he is fatefully subject (so that it cannot be charged to his account).[30]

This, I hope, has made it clear what I meant by the introduction of Docetism into anthropology. That term points to the ultimate theological reason why the listener says, "That sermon did not have anything to do with me."

So when a sermon does not "hit home," the reason need by no means lie in the fact that it contained no examples from life nor that it was too theoretical. On the contrary, despite all its rhetorical and pedagogical excellences, it may lie in the fact that the preacher is speaking on the basis of a Docetic anthropology and that the man of whom he is speaking and whom he is addressing does not appear in the sermon at all. Then the very hearers who are troubled by very real situational problems feel that they have been bypassed. And perhaps the only ones who listen are those who are largely removed from the worldly situation—the old people who have withdrawn from life. (Note that we said "largely," not "altogether." For even an old folks' home still exhibits the structure of the world in miniature, just as did the monastery cell into which Luther took his terrors and his world.)

The unfortunate and unhealthy preponderance of older people in our services of worship therefore cannot be changed by starting special projects for the young and the middle-aged and discussing their problems. When this is done—and why shouldn't it be done? —some good work is certainly accomplished, and here the Evangelical Academies deserve special praise. But if this is the *only* thing that is done, the result is the formation of Christian cell groups, academy associations, and many other organizations which may be welcome, but it has no effect upon the main service of worship. And if we are not completely deceived, the situation that largely obtains today is that the 5 per cent of the population who attend church and who besides are confined to certain ages do not constitute a representative cross-section of Christians, nor are they the sole remaining relics of Christianity in our country. The majority even of so-called vital Christians—God save the mark—are living outside the services of worship. This statistical distortion can be changed only by changing the theological foundation of our preaching, namely, by ceasing to be Docetists.

The Triumph of Disengagement and Boredom

If I were to say quite briefly how we got on to this disastrous road to Docetism, I would leave out of account any attempt to analyze the history of theology, though this could contribute something to our insight. I therefore refrain from examining in more detail the existentialistic sources of this false theology and from going back to Kierkegaard and even further. I shall content myself with making this practical observation: *The disaster of Docetism has arisen from the fact that we leap from the text into the sermon without having traversed the field of ethics.* Here, of course, I mean by ethics not simply moral theology but an interpretation by means of Christian categories of reality, which is to say, man's being-in-the-world.

The reader may pardon here a personal observation which may illustrate what I mean. After the appearance of the first volumes of my "Theological Ethics" and a number of volumes of sermons I noted that, apart from a few exceptions, the readers of the scientific work paid no attention to the sermon books and vice versa. Among those who knew about the other "department" the kindly disposed thought they could detect a certain versatility in extremely different fields. I hardly ever noted, however, that anybody had even noticed the *inner* connection between the two areas of work. Actually I wrote the "Ethics" in order to do the theological background work for preaching. I attempted to interpret what man is in his worldly reality and thus to explore the various areas of his existence: the world of autonomisms and boundary situations, the world of politics and business, sexuality, and art. I sought to catch the law and the gospel, judgment and grace, in the particular refraction that resulted when the divine light fell upon the many-sided prism of human existence. Only so, I felt, could I find the way out of Docetism—though at first this particular theme was approached only instinctively and then later became more and more clearly a matter of reflection. Thus the work on the "Ethics" helped me to preach (and vice versa!). I do not know whether Wolfgang Trillhaas had a similar experience.[31] In any case, it has always struck me as significant that this distinguished preacher and homiletician likewise found the way to ethics as his first great systematic work.

To this personal observation I may add, again as an illustration, another recollection of a sermon which I heard preached. I made notes on it because it struck me as being a melancholy model of Docetic remoteness from the world. This impression was intensified even more by the fact that the ideas in it seemed to be self-generated and kept revolving in a void. This could hardly have been otherwise because here the gospel was removed from any polarity whatsoever with reality and thus delivered over to an empty flow of words. Here are the notes I wrote on this sermon:

Text: "Darkness shall cover the earth, and thick darkness the peoples" (Isa. 60:2, RSV).

"Do we not feel the darkness lying over the earth? Darkness, wherever we look—east, west, north, south, nearby and far away . . . ? Are not the peoples fearful and hopeless, but individuals too? Who can say that there is no darkness around him?" So it went on for a long time. The preacher kept on, as it were, mixing dark colors, but one could not see any forms or figures emerging from it. The preacher himself generated a vague and confused darkness, a night in which all cats are gray. The monotony, the melancholy clatter of words, simply forced the hearer to turn off his mind, so that he was not even put in a position to draw the associations and applications to his own life which the sermon failed to do. Perhaps before he was overpowered with sleep he may have thought, with one last protest, that, after all, his life was certainly not *that* dark. His job gave him some satsifaction and, once he got through this hour in church, he would hear the laughter of his children. At any rate, in this negative part of the sermon there was nothing more than wallowing about in this "darkness." The positive part was really much worse—probably because the real gospel stands out in such drastic contrast to this Docetic pallidity that it becomes a judgment: "But over the darkness dawns the light. The gospel means the coming of light. The gospel means to have hope. Christians are waiting, expectant people. Christians are people who go to meet the future. All men would like to hope. But here is real hope. I say to you at this Advent season that there is hope. The church would not be the church if it were to give up the slightest bit of this hope. Here we must speak out fully and solidly, here we dare not give an inch; otherwise we shall not be able to stand before the nihilists of our time. The church is and remains the church of hope . . . ," etc., etc., etc.

I have a rubber stamp which reads "Why?" which I often use to mark the margins of students' papers. I would have liked to use this rubber stamp on this sermon. The words "We dare not give an inch" were spoken in a tone of great firmness and resolution, with the passion of a great confessor. But just what this *was* that produced this hope of ours and keeps it alive in spite of the reality of the world, he never did say. It was as if the preacher were constantly saying, "Here I stand, I cannot do otherwise," but forgot to say what it was he was standing on and what he could not do otherwise. The listener was left hopelessly behind and so he took refuge in sleep. And the man I am quoting is not a "little man," but a fairly well-known light of the church in a medium-sized city in West Germany. Nor was it merely a lapse on the part of a man who was possibly tired from overwork. When I listened to him again on a later visit to check my impression, the preaching was exactly the same. The complexion of the audience was the same too.

I need not add that this is an extremely negative example. It would be dreadful if we were obliged to make the general statement that this is what sermons are today. No, they really are not. We always tend to use extremes as illustrations. But in this extreme we can discern dangers which lie in wait for all of us who stand in the pulpit. This is why this warning signal is raised.

We still hear the reproach of "pulpit tone" and "pulpit passion" uttered by critics outside of the church; but this is fatuous. The booming pathos of the unctuous bore is hardly ever heard any more. It would be interesting to find out why it is that preachers have obviously broken off this habit. Our danger lies elsewhere. It lies in that nonproductive flow of words which is no longer geared into real life as men live it and only makes people say, "There's nothing there for me" or "This never touched me at all." It does not even elicit a protest, it does not even offend. Only boredom triumphs. Boredom is the psychological effect of what we mean by the theological term "Docetism."

Unfortunately it cannot be said that academic theology as it is taught by not a few theologians and formulated in not a few publications offers any remedy. Here too the situation is that frequently (though, thank heaven, not always) we find men living on esoteric problems which crop up in the theologians' conversation among themselves, that, as we said above, they keep on chasing, chiseling, and scholastically refining but hardly ever bring forth a new idea, or they get mired down in methodological considerations and disappear in the smoke of hermeneutics. As Karl Rahner has said, they keep on refining their methods and constantly sharpening their knives but no longer have anything to carve.

The Flight into Busywork and Liturgical Artcraft

If the preaching situation has become as muddled and confused as we have felt it necessary to describe it, and if some very painful operations on the theological root are necessary to overcome it, it is quite human and understandable that men will seek to evade the difficulty and choose the path of least resistance. There are not a few of such paths which are no doubt identical with what Jesus calls the "broad way." One way out is to throw oneself into the hectic business of "running" a congregation, the busyness that sucks up all one's energy and creates the illusion that one is consuming oneself in the service of the kingdom of God. There is also the crazy mania for traveling: in Japan there is an international conference on children's worship (as if this could not be taken care of by an exchange of experience through brochures and a few air-mail letters); in Canada there is a meeting of some world federation or other. Many are only passive participants in such sessions, merely casting their ballots; and again and again a resolution has to be revised so that everybody will be satisfied. But everybody has the illusion that he is serving the "world-wide church." Humanly speaking, this is very pleasant, because one is always meeting the same old familiar faces. And at home the hard task of day-by-day ministry is left undone (all for the sake, of course, of the alleged "greater work of the church"!). But a flood of reports will be read—about the last conference and what it demands of us, or about the next conference and what we may expect from it. Then you fly back home again to repack your bag for another junket. In the process the onerous task of boring into the hard wood of sermon preparation is forgotten.

That may sound provocative; and it should! We have no right to talk in generalizations here either. I know men who are quite properly at work on this level and whose service is necessary. But I also see the many "fellow travelers," the backbenchers, the filling and padding of the conferences. I see the shirking and the choosing of the easier path. And I think not only of the flocks without a shepherd, fed only intermittently and with no proper care—there are professors too who are always on the road, cutting their classes or leaving them to assistants—but also of how many hungry Indian children could be fed with the travel expenses.

Please understand me rightly. Naturally I am not attacking the ecumenical relationships of the church and the institutions which are needed to cultivate them. I am only criticizing a particular form of this sterile, nonproductive busyness, which all too clearly reveals the motive of flight and the "least resistance." As a small boy I wanted to be a missionary. Only later did I realize that what animated me was less the desire to convert the heathen than to eat bananas. Even grown folks can sometimes deceive themselves concerning their motives. Foreign lands are alluring, interconfessional conversations are fascinating, and fraternal meetings with fellow believers are refreshing. It is a fine thing that all this is added unto us when we have some serious work to do in foreign lands. And there is no commandment of God which demands that we must fight down the desire for a change of scene and adventure so that only the chemically pure desire to serve and a cramped and rigid selflessness is left. Our motives are very complex, and why shouldn't they be? If I had actually become a missionary, I probably would not have been ashamed of the fact that the lust for bananas played a part in my choice of vocation. Of course, if I had to recognize that it was the bananas which were the real treasure on which my heart was set, I would have been honestly dismayed. All our Christian sovereignty over our multiple motives and all our childlike trust in him who knows our hearts and will be a merciful judge obviously cannot exempt us from the task of searching our hearts and facing the self-critical question of where the real center of our motives lies. And if in ecumenical meetings the real motive turns out to be flight and aversion from faithfulness in the small tasks, if this should be the point where a very worldly "tourism" breaks into the church, then there is nothing for it but to repent and turn around.

Not that we should *neglect* the cultivation of contacts and encounters! The Body of Christ must be constantly re-experiencing its oneness in all its many members and also in all its geographical dimensions. The only question is whether this task could not be met in quite other ways. My own experiences in a fairly large number of countries have led me to the view that one should send to other churches and other parts of the world men and women who will perform under ecumenical auspices certain *tasks,* such as preaching, lecturing, helping to establish institutions. We learn to know one another only by working together in a common cause. Then the ecumenical bond of love will be added unto us, as a byproduct, as it were, of the really central thing. It cannot, however, be secured directly. We cannot make a vocation of openness and receptiveness to others. The result of that is sterility and self-deception. Then we arrive at the false dream, of the "world-wide church," which in truth is only the outlying meeting place for functionaries and the practice field for bureaucratic apparatus.

The most hidden path of least resistance is perhaps the flight into "liturgism" which is becoming epidemic among us. I purposely avoid speaking of flight into the liturgy, but rather speak of an evasive maneuver into "liturgism." This does not mean that I am against the liturgy itself, but rather against a particular pathologically hypertrophic emphasis upon it. I am not contending against the liturgy itself, but rather against a particular motive which prompts some to promote it. More precisely expressed, it is a matter of a *number* of motives which must be viewed critically.

In the first place, as has been said, it is a flight from preaching. Men are faced with a necessity—which is that the work of preaching is simply too hard for them—and they proceed to make a virtue of it by saying that their aim is to overcome subjectivity in the church. They foster a set order which must be performed according to the formulary and the rubrics. Often this is accompanied by a great deal of solemn play-acting, dressing up in liturgical vestments, and wanderings to and fro from the epistle side of the altar to the gospel side, from the altar to the lectern, pulpit, and the sanctuary rail. We are regaled with symbolisms, synthetically contrived or borrowed from Catholicism. And what may be genuine in Catholicism—because it is based upon an unbroken tradition—strikes us as artificial and affected. A small circle of artsy-craftsy dilettantes may find satisfaction in it, perhaps even spiritual satisfaction. But anyone who comes from the outside to this kind of thing (and after all, ought we not to be compelling them to come in from the streets and market places!) will as a rule be helplessly lost and can hardly respond to it. The esoteric congregation may find spiritual nourishment in it, but it forgets the immeasurable multitudes outside. Here the love of the shepherd for those who have strayed will easily grow cold. And one may also lose one's sense of the proportion between the secularized, forsaken masses and the little "core congregation." How horrible that one should think one has done something for the kingdom of God by introducing liturgical vestments! As I said once before, it often looks as if the Word of God has emigrated from the text into textiles.

It was no less a person than Dietrich Bonhoeffer who in the midst of the horrors of the Third Reich, when confessing one's faith and therefore preaching was peculiarly difficult, recognized this flight into liturgism and suggested that many were seeking

here a stormproof zone where they could be secure and not have
to expose themselves to harsh encounters with sinners. He too did
not reject the necessity of working on the liturgy and renewing it,
but he did say, "Only he who cries out for the Jews dare permit
himself to sing in Gregorian."[32] He thereby blocked the potential
escapist's path.

The second motive we stand against is the purism and the legalism with which these people operate. Just as Docetism appears
to have an "indelible character" and merely changes its form and
the place where it manifests itself, so the same seems to be true of
legalism. Even among the advocates of the gospel and justification
by faith alone (both of which, after all, are dead set *against* legalism) it can suddenly become virulent again and wear the mask of
"order."

In Lutheranism, of all places, but certainly not confined to it, in
Germany and in the United States, a rage for regulations, rubrics,
and orders has erupted, literally overlaying life, worship, and doctrine with laws. And how legalistic and puristic this legalism is!
The liturgiologists and the church musicologists, very learned and
nice people, to be sure, proceed to show us all the treasures which
we have lost during the course of the centuries, how much Rationalism and "Nineteenth Century" there still is among us, how many
hymns have been badly modernized and "improved" and how
many tunes have been botched. So they apply their archaeology
and restore the past to its pristine perfection, while consigning the
present to the devil.

The Dominion of the Purists and Antiquarians

I address myself to the German situation, but I know what has
gone on here is also true of liturgical revisions elsewhere. The
purists and antiquarians have restored the old forms of speech.
What do they care whether anybody understands what they mean!
Look at the prayers in the first volume of the new liturgy and

you will get linguistic creeps, and the missionary gets a blow below the belt.

In the Reformation era the iconoclasts were suspect, but today the "hymnoclasts" seem to be the fair-haired boys of the church. For generations the hymnbook has been given to people not only for singing but for praying; generations have nourished their hearts upon it. But now the treasure house has been plundered and filled with ostensibly "more genuine" treasures. The tunes have been altered. You begin to sing a hymn quite innocently and manfully, and suddenly you are thrown into a deep pit, you hit a low note where before there was a high one. And the words too have been "restored" to their original form, because the small clique of connoisseurs wants it that way and the minority tyrannizes over the rest of us. And the language becomes so archaic that footnotes must be added to explain what the words mean. What a chore it is to sing a hymn these days. You not only have to follow the music exactly in order not to expose yourself as a musical nonconformist, but you must at the same time study the text and keep descending into the cellar to consult the footnotes. There are even some modern hymn writers who provide their effusions with the desired patina, and so their hymns too must be furnished with footnotes. And naturally hymns like "*Harre, meine Seele*" ("Wait on God, and trust Him") and "*So nimm denn meine Hände*" ("Take Thou my hand and lead me") are denoted with a star, which, as you know, in the hymnbook means the opposite of what it does in Baedeker; it means that the hymn "is not suitable for use in the chief service." In other words, it receives no decent burial among the saints but is consigned to the cemetery for suicides. What does it matter to these liturgical aesthetes that people have been comforted by these hymns, that they have died with these words on their lips, and that they learned to love these verses in the hardest hours of their lives!

Here I cannot refrain from telling a brief anecdote. Some years ago I went to a refugee camp with a number of my students to give some help to the poorest of the poor. We preached in the small camp chapel and held evening devotions in the corridors. We assisted the new arrivals with their baggage and the filling out of innumerable forms and tried to comfort them in their despair. They were difficult days and they demanded a great deal of the students and also of me. Every day I gathered the students together to listen to their experiences and to give them some human and spiritual encouragement.

In the evenings we met with those who were to be "shipped out" the next day (often after weeks, months, or even years in the camp) and would now have to make a new start in life. For them it was extremely exciting; they were filled with anxiety and also with hope. After one of us had spoken, they were asked to choose a hymn we might sing together. And what do you think?—with almost predictable regularity they chose *"Harre, meine Seele"* or *"So nimm denn meine Hände."* The first time it happened I was a bit edgy, for I was visualizing what was going on in the minds of some of my young friends. Some of them were in fact a bit puristic in matters liturgical. They will suffer aesthetic torments, I thought, if they not only have to listen to these hymns but even sing them themselves. I expected to see some pained faces when the first one was announced. But they sang lustily, simply because they were sorry for these people and their sharing of their hard life had enabled them to identify with them.

But then they saw how these people were gripped and moved; they began to see what these hymns could mean to these people in their hard situation. They even saw tears and they could not bring themselves to dismiss it all as "sentimentality." They were also touched by the devotion with which the very ones whom they knew to be believing Christians sang. And suddenly these young liturgical aesthetes suffered a change: they began to like these hymns. Not because their aesthetic judgment about them had suddenly changed! This had not changed at all. But because they saw that the aesthetic category is inappropriate here or that this category is not capable of elucidating the mystery of what was happening here.

These hymns were suddenly freighted with the faith, hope, and devotion of those who sang them. Therefore, all at once they were not just sentimental chaff, but had weight and consequence. It was as if they had been justified by the faith of those who were edified by them, as if they had received a kind of "alien righteousness" (and therefore not their own aesthetic righteousness). In our discussion sessions the students themselves spoke to me about the curious change in their attitude and wondered what the reason for it was. I then talked to them about the alien righteousness which we human beings too receive, the righteousness which is proclaimed by those verses which are both a hymn and a children's prayer:

> Jesus, thy Blood and Righteousness
> My beauty are, my glorious dress;
> 'Midst flaming worlds, in these arrayed,
> With joy shall I lift up my head.

This alien righteousness can also be imparted to our hymns. It can even adhere to the often dubious offerings of money we make. It can even be imparted to aesthetic horrors of some neogothic churches. Are not even these churches mysteriously transformed when they are filled with a congregation at prayer? Is not their architectural nakedness then covered as it were with the beauty and glorious dress of which that hymn speaks? But then do we have the right simply to dismiss with contempt what has been hallowed by faith and love, merely because we have the cheek to judge it only by aesthetic standards?

It might be different if these manipulations and spoliations could at least be explained by the desire to give Protestant Christianity a common hymnal and a common form of worship. It is true, of course, that even this kind of unity must not be overrated, for variety too has its place—and its appeal—in the kingdom of God. All the same, however, there is something pleasant in finding the same community of the Father's house even in externals in every place I visit, and I would grant that people might be expected to give up some of the things that are loved and familiar. But the manipulations of the purists not only go very much further but they are also determined by many other motives, for example, the passion for the historic and the preservation of monuments. One might perhaps concede this motive also, though we cannot ignore its dubiousness. But then if they could only let things grow, instead of organizing, rubricating, and decreeing them! It is as if they wanted to recover in a few years by way of rationalized planning and official directives what took centuries to grow in the Catholic Church. But when our passion is given to these things how can we go out and search for the lost and strayed and how can we help losing our feeling for the deserts and the thorns into which they have strayed? Is not all this liturgical preoccupation a gigantic production in which the church has lost sight of the real tasks and the one thing needful? Could not the whole experiment bring down upon us the judgment: "Take away from me the noise of your songs; to the melody of your harps I will not listen"?[33]

The Perversion of the Protestant Principle

I too am of the opinion that the hymns we mentioned are not classical chorales. I do not wish to create the impression that I am defending the thesis that it is a matter of indifference whether things liturgical meet the rigorous requirements of taste and workmanlike order. Anybody who makes such radical demands of the preacher, even in matters of form, will hardly be willing to tolerate slovenliness in the other areas of the service of worship. But to be strict in all these matters does not rule out that one may distinguish various degrees not only of spiritual but also of aesthetic maturity, that one may admit that there are various stages of development and not merely the ultimate stage of an inveterate, dyed-in-the-wool liturgiologist. Isn't it possible to let things grow

—and at the same time have some love and respect for those who are in a previous stage of development?

After all, the gospel means that we have to find man where he is. The messengers who were sent out to invite men to the royal banquet were told to go out into the highways and hedges and market places. People do not have to be already wearing wedding garments in order to be invited. They were met and brought in while they were still wearing rags. God turns up beside them and Christ eats with sinners. Would he be embarrassed to eat with those who sin in matters aesthetic? Would he wince and shudder if he heard the hymns of The Salvation Army, the "gospel songs," and some of the sentimental tunes of the nineteenth century? Is he partial only to Gregorian sung in cathedrals? We have nothing against Gregorian or liturgical dress (though it is questionable whether they ultimately contribute to the communication of the gospel to modern man), but we are certainly against flopping over to this kind of thing too soon. In the highways and hedges, before the protocol and formality of the wedding feast takes over, all this seems quite strange, and back on the streets people do not recognize each other in this fancy dress. Anybody who conducts missions in the Hamburg tenderloin (*Reeperbahn*) knows that he cannot ask people to sing "A mighty fortress is our God." But Christianity is far too richly gifted not to have the appropriate wardrobe, properties, and settings also for those who are on the outside.

If I see aright, this overleaping of the various stages of development is the negative consequence of a Protestant principle. The Reformation began with a threefold absolute: man is justified by faith alone, by grace alone, and only on the basis of the Holy Scriptures. And here again we see the same thing that occurred in the case of our language: in the course of secularization this absolute became formalized and was elevated into a general principle, even a law that governed our style of thinking. Then Protestant means to be "absolute" and to think only in terms of either-or.

I am not certain that it is so, but it sometimes appears to me as if this formalized law of the absolute is beginning to work itself out today in matters of liturgy. It then expresses itself in the kind of purism which we have described, which insists upon having the optimal historical form of worship and therefore forgets to address itself to those who must be sought out at totally different levels. The person who is puristically concerned with the absolute, the unconditional, always takes his stand on principles, and therefore is no longer able to love. For the precondition of love is that one must have regard for what is different from oneself. (And this regard is fostered in the school of Jesus Christ.) But the puristic absolutist is also no longer free, but rather slavishly bound to his perfectionism, even in the realm of liturgy. And therefore in the last analysis he also has no sense of humor. He can no longer laugh. At most he can only indulge in ironical laughter over the queer flowers which the tree of the kingdom of God produces, the strange excrescences that grow rampant, and the peculiar eccentricities of human beings. He laughs at everything except himself. And instead of rejoicing over God's rich palette he goes on drawing his straight line, fastidiously and captiously determining what lies inside and outside the pale.

At this point how much more evangelical, because less pedantic and punctilious on principle, is the Catholic Church, which exercises only a cautious control even over the more extravagant excrescences of popular piety and can tolerate not only a Romano Guardini but also a Pater Leppich. Here one is not constantly confronted with an either-or, the decision of "all or nothing." Here there is the disposition to let things grow and at the same time to show love for what remains aesthetically or intellectually stunted or does not get beyond a very reduced standard. In the place of *decision* (as a principle!) what we have here is *education*, a real evangelical concern to seek out people in the streets or in the open fields where perhaps before only pantheism has flourished.

I am well aware that this can contain not only virtues but also vices: compromises, concessions, tactical expediencies, opportunism, indecision, and many half-measures. I also know that the Catholic principle of *analogia entis* provides a very questionable basic presupposition to enable one to make a relatively easy point of contact with the given. But I do not concede that evangelical Christianity on the basis of *its* presuppositions does not have available the same possibility of contact and growth. For the New Testament is full of references of this kind. I need only refer to the pericope of the woman with an issue of blood whom Jesus healed and whose faith he praised.[34] This pitiful woman lived under the spell of a magical conception of the world. She believed that she would be healed through physical contact with a fetish (for her this is what the Man of Nazareth was). So she touched the hem of his garment. She obviously had no conception of his message. Perhaps she had not even seen his face and had no knowledge of his "personality." For she "came up behind him in the crowd," and thus proceeded furtively, seeking only to gain a magical contact.

I can imagine how a liturgical perfectionist or an ecclesiastic with the standard Lutheran theology would react to this situation. And I have some hesitations about describing this situation because for the reasons we have mentioned, there is in these circles very little sense of humor and certainly very little willingness to laugh at oneself. At the risk of again causing indignation, I would characterize the reaction to be expected as follows: "My dear woman, the presuppositions under which you seek contact with me are not legitimate. [Perhaps he would be nice enough to go on and explain these rather difficult words to this unschooled woman.] I am not one of the saviours in your magical world; I am a man with a message. First you must know what the message is and decide about it before we can go on talking. So first you must be willing to submit to the correction of your wrong presuppositions. You will have to attend some classes before I can give my placet to your desire to be healed and call your faith 'great' and 'legitimate.' "

But Christ acted quite differently from the way the lights of his church would presumably act. He accepted the woman with all the dubious immaturity of her faith, healed her, and acknowledged her faith—without criticism. He met her in the midst of her magical world; before he complied with her plea he did not insist upon putting her into a course of catechetical re-education. He certainly would also have accepted her if she had approached him chanting. But the kind of chanting she would have done at this stage would surely have given an aesthetic liturgist the creeps.

What later became of the people whom Jesus met—the Canaanite woman, the publican Zacchaeus, the rich young ruler, and the woman with an issue of blood—is left to Christian imagination. Probably the sticklers for principle in our circles would regard this exercise of the imagination as a frivolous undertaking. Nevertheless I would like to hang on to this imagined picture for a moment, especially since the sticklers will have long since hung up. I imagine that this woman who was so unexpectedly healed continued to follow her Saviour and that in further association with him she not only saw him from behind but also face to face, indeed, that she was filled with curiosity (not with a curiosity about salvation—my imagination does not run that far!)—about what this Man had to say and what his actions would tell her about him. And as she kept on following him, simply because she had been so puzzlingly and mysteriously accepted by him, she more and more grew out of her magical enthrallment and into a real discipleship.

This would be growth, education, this would be meeting people where they are. This would be freedom to give oneself to people. This would be love. This story should help us to grow out of our bondage to principles.

The Pseudo-sacred

Liturgical purism has, it seems to me, another fault. It appears to me that it grossly contradicts what we have otherwise completely accepted as a theological tenet. It is almost a commonplace of our conviction that there is no such thing as a separation between the sacred and the profane. And we know how frequently Dietrich Bonhoeffer is cited as a patron saint of this thesis. Naturally this opens up a broad field of problems which we cannot enter here. Besides, the thesis itself is not as clear as it appears to be. And if we inquire more closely into what is meant by Bonhoeffer's formula, the nonreligious interpretation of the kerygma and worldly Christianity, we shall not be much wiser. Hence the scramble of wild interpretations in this area. The likelihood is, it seems to me, that the legitimate core of this thesis lies in the fact that it draws definite consequences from the Reformation doctrine of justification.

That is to say, if our justification occurs "by faith alone," then salvation is a matter of believing or not believing. Then, in any case, there can be no quantitative approaches to salvation by means of merits, by lifting the level of our accomplishments. On the contrary, then our salvation is completely independent of these quantitative differences. Therefore the negative statement, "not by works," is linked with the positive statement, "by faith alone."

And connected with this rejection of any meritorious and quantitative approach to salvation is also the rejection of any institutional forms of approach. There can, for example, be no places, vocations, and institutions selected out of the world which are nearer to salvation and in a comparative sense "holier" than others. Thus there can be no priesthood elevated above the world and no monasteries which can claim the peculiar prerogatives of holiness. Just as justifying faith reduces "works" to one level as far as salvation is concerned, so it levels all institutions and places on earth.

It was in this way that Luther's idea of the worldly worship of God arose: the maid who wields a broom and the mother who bears her children are serving God through their worldly work when they do it in faith. The sacral privileges cease to exist, including the clerical privileges, for now the spiritual office no longer stands upon the church, but it is rather the church—as the Body of Christ in the world—which ordains men to this office.

Nor in the strict sense are these any sacral places which are set apart from the world by special consecrations. Wherever these are mentioned in the context of the Reformation faith they can be understood only as "signs" and "pointers," but not as places having a superior ontic quality. And only within these bounds can there be any sense in cultivating a special sacral style, as, for example, in the building of churches.

As we said above, these consequences of the Reformation doctrine of justification seem to me to constitute the core of the thesis that there must be no fundamental dividing wall between the sacred and the profane, and that therefore the message of the Word become flesh must be spoken in *worldly* terms, that it must meet people where they are.

However many unsolved problems await us here, there is one thing that is sure, and that is that liturgism is in a fair way of re-erecting that dividing wall and sealing off an esoteric realm of the sacral. I need not here go into detail in describing the exaggeration of ceremonial, which is the expression of this tendency.

Perhaps I may illustrate what I mean by this segregation of the sacral by telling of an experience I had in a Christian student camp in California. One evening we gathered for a jolly dinner at which the youngsters all wore fancy, homemade hats. At such a semi-carnival party held by Christians in our country the table prayer would have been omitted for reasons of taste. Not so here; all these comically adorned heads bowed in reverence! But then came something more surprising. While we were eating several quartets sang religious songs set to popular-style music. In astonishment I asked them why they did this and the reply was: "These are Christian recreation songs. Do you think that is strange? Why should we allow Christ to be with us only in moments of worship and exclude him in our hours of relaxation? In these hours of recreation why shouldn't we borrow these things from other people who do not know him?"

I am not saying that this is exemplary and recommending that it be emulated. Probably our sense of propriety in these matters, to which we have become inured by long tradition, would rebel against it. But here there was a melody, sung in an *American* key, for which we ought to find a counterpart. Here, without any regard for what might be lost, without any inhibitions born of inbred laws of taste and style, the dividing wall between the sacred and the profane was torn down; this was "worldly" proclamation, American-style. Here, in a questionably modern and American way, was what once also existed among us. For in our past too there were times when our spiritual and secular songs were not yet, or in any case not fundamentally, separated from each other.

It should not be thought that I am overlooking the dangers and the risks in all this: the lurking latent secularization, the threat of the pastor's being reduced to the role of administrator and entertainer, the possible degeneration of the church into a social organization. The practice of truths—and here a truth *was* perceivable!—is never possible without a calculated risk. Indeed, even the enunciation of theological truths involves a risk. As we said above, heresies must be ventured in order to gain truths. Those who live only by sealing themselves off are in the end left with only empty husks which no longer contain any truth at all. Everything is dangerous. Even the Sermon on the Mount is dangerous; it can turn a man into a visionary fanatic. The doctrine of justification is dangerous; it can turn a man into a libertine who flouts obedience because, after all, if he has faith nothing can happen to him. He who deals with the truth is always letting himself in for danger. But he also has the promise that in the truth he will not perish but rather that it will make him free.

Now, after having had to say all these critical things about liturgism, it is important that we characterize briefly the true purpose of the liturgy and see it in proportion.

The Liturgy and the Sermon

The first and foremost purpose of the liturgy seems to me to be that of allowing the assembled congregation to be the acting subject of the service of worship and accordingly to allow it to participate in worship. After all, it is the congregation that prays, praises God, gives thanks to him, puts the eternal Word in the center of things, and responds to it. The office of the preacher does not stand over against the congregation but is rather established in its midst; it is assigned, or better, delegated, to the minister by the church. The congregation is by no means an audience that remains passive while it is being preached at. The purpose of the liturgy is to give expression to the action of the congregation. All liturgical forms are to be judged by the criterion of whether and to what extent they are capable of doing this and, beyond this, of doing it properly. The mere activation of the congregation in speaking and singing alone is, of course, not sufficient. The words and the singing must be such that the congregation can make them its own, not something which is decreed or imposed upon it. Otherwise the result is only a veiled form of passivity and a variant of what is called "infused faith" in Roman Catholic theology.

The second function of the liturgy is that it constitutes a stationary element nourished by tradition and thus has complementary significance for the sermon.

The sermon must be contemporary, it must correspond with the time in which it is preached; it is linked with the venture of the witness who trusts the Spirit who moves where he wills. It is true that the witness is given a text; but to interpret and address and contemporize it, this is the business of the witness, at any rate his business in the sense that he puts himself at the service of God's business. It is possible for a sermon, just because it may contain ventures and therefore risks too (because, for one thing, it must deal with alienation), to go wrong or strike the wrong note. Its level may also vary. It also depends to some extent upon the situation of the preacher, his experiences, his vigor or his weariness, his spiritual and human disposition. The degree of theological insight and human maturity also plays a part. And finally, the contributing influence of the spirit of the times, both theological and otherwise, must not be underestimated. It is this influence above all which makes it possible to speak of there being a "history of preaching." Anybody who reads collections of sermons from the past observes immediately that none of what is said in them can be brought into the pulpit unchanged today, even though it may be the work of very great preachers whose names are still known.

It is true, however, that we sometimes hear sermons today which might have been preached in 1880. But this seeming timelessness indicates, not an excellence, but rather a degeneration of preaching. When it consists of the mere citation of biblical and liturgical idioms and only strings the traditional beads in new combinations, it is impossible to make a theological error, and the same thing can be done a hundred years from now. The impression of timelessness can be achieved only by ignoring one's own time and never allowing the Word to become flesh. Therefore such a sermon could have been preached back in 1880. But probably even then it would not have lured a dog from behind a warm stove, as Luther puts it, any more than it does today when it is being delivered.

Therefore the fact that preaching is bound to its time and reflects its times is not the disadvantage but rather the virtue of preaching (assuming that it does not merely accommodate itself to its time and therefore become indistinguishable from it). The preacher owes the ultimate message only to *his* time. And when he has run his course, he hands the torch on to others.

But because the sermon is a risk, even an adventure, it needs the corrective of the liturgy and the stationary element that is inherent in it. Here the Holy Scriptures are read and the ancient prayers of the church are said. Here are the responses which have become the common treasure of the church, at any rate when artificially introduced or produced in the form of liturgical art-craft. Here alongside of the voice of the venturing witness is the superpersonal voice, the "we," of the church which has sounded through the centuries. To quote Dietrich Bonhoeffer again, "Where the *cantus firmus* is clear and distinct, the counterpoint can be developed as mightily as possible. Both are "unmingled and yet separated," to use the words of the Chalcedonian formula, like Christ in his divine and his human nature."[35] The *cantus firmus* is the liturgy and the counterpoint is the sermon: the sermon can swing out in a wide arc, it can be venturesome. Thus the service of worship is an integral, indivisible whole.

When I come to the period of Rationalism in my course on the history of theology I always derive a certain amusement out of presenting to my students examples of Rationalistic preaching. These reverend gentlemen spoke about many things in those days, but hardly about the Word of God. They talked about the advantages of pure air, about troubles with cattle and husbandry in general, and about many topics under the head of the art of living. If there had been nothing else but the sermon, Christianity would probably have been preached to death. But in the liturgies the ancient texts were read, sometimes even there a bit watered down and "improved," but nevertheless . . . Often enough the text fitted the sermon like a square peg in a round hole, and yet it was there, even though in a moment it seemed to be almost completely smothered by the sermonizing and certainly for the most part was not understood. And yet that which remained hidden in incubation within the texts one day sprang to life again. The dry stalk that lay over the winter in the cellar of the liturgy suddenly put forth shoots of green and the day came when a new and vital preaching rejoined the liturgy. The gravestone of a degenerated preaching was not strong enough to keep the living among the dead. An "idea" could not have survived such treatment; but in the keep of the liturgy the Risen Christ was waiting for his new day.

This is the promise of the liturgy. The fact that it thus constitutes the stationary element in public worship cannot, of course, mean that it can be allowed to become uninhibitedly antiquarian and that people do not need to understand it. Superannuated forms of words which cannot be assimilated and cannot become the "Word" today do not "tune" people in but rather out. As far as the liturgy is concerned, to be the representative of the constant and stationary means something quite different from passing on ancient forms and labels whose meaning is no longer understood. Therefore the liturgy too requires careful correction and modernizations. But these will be only variations and paraphrases of the abiding, the permanent. And this abiding element the hearers who are present will receive into themselves, and through them it will become a present reality. For it is precisely as the abiding element that the liturgy should pass over into the flesh and blood of the actual, present church. But it can do this only on two conditions, first that it be understood, and second, that it be constantly repeated, from childhood to old age, that it become as familiar as the voice of one's mother.

And this is exactly why I think it is so disastrous that the liturgiologists keep changing the existing liturgies and allow the familiar things to die, that even the hymnals are subjected to radical—and actually very dubious—operations. The business is by no means made any better, but at best becomes only a sad

paradox, when we are told that these revisions have been under-
taken in the interest of restoring the past perfect, when we find
ancient, long-forgotten treasures dragged out and heaped upon
people in the form of new liturgical enrichments. (The people
have enough heaped on their plates in other ways too; for example, who can digest three Scripture lessons in one service?) The
continuity which is entrusted to the liturgy can be destroyed not
only by being too progressive but also by being reactionary. It
does not make much difference whether stages are skipped going
forward or going backward; the work of destruction is done either
way.

Not that we have anything against the ancient treasures! But, as
we said, one must be able to let things grow, because it is only the
devil who has no time. To hang some pictures differently and to
add others carefully and at due intervals is quite another thing
from iconoclasm.

The spiritual and the psychological consequences of the destruction of the familiar are tremendous. Therefore the congregations must be stirred to resist this trend. I confess, however, that I
do not entertain any excessive hopes in this matter. If I see the
situation aright (I may be deceiving myself, but I do not think
so), the reactionary tendencies in things liturgical and in antiquarian confessionalism are strongest in the territorial churches in
which secularism is most rampant and in which the congregations
have dwindled to a small percentage of the total population. Here
even the Christians live pretty largely outside the services of worship. And one can hardly expect the miserable remnant of church
attendants—we have already spoken of its composition—to recognize the hour of danger and rouse itself to great effort. All the
more reason, then, that some strong words be addressed to the
consciences of the responsible church authorities. They must not
bow to the dictation of the esoteric clique.

Complete the Reformation or Recatholicization?

Let us not deceive ourselves. The alternative which we face—precisely in view of the liturgical situation—can be set forth in the following questions:

Does Protestantism have any future at all or must we honestly confess that we have come to the end of the road? Despite all the trumpeting at Reformation seasons has it perhaps been only four hundred years of salutary fever in the body of the Catholic Church? Has this body perhaps now thrown off certain scoriae and poisons, which enables it to undergo a regeneration? And is the Vatican Council in Rome perhaps the sign of a healthy convalescence which the restored organism—that body which has not only eliminated toxic matter but has also imbibed certain truth-drugs from the Reformation witness—is now experiencing? Was the Evangelical church perhaps nothing more than a gigantic interim? Was it only a historical incident whose time has now run out? It would be dishonest of me to act as if these were merely rhetorical questions and leave you with the implied answer that this is not so and that we are actually just beginning a new day that beckons us to new shores.

Sometimes I really ask myself whether all this may not be true after all, whether we are perhaps on our way to a homecoming. And in all conscience I do not know whether this question is grounded in unbelief and discouragement or in expectation of a secret promise.

I see that the Catholic Church, despite all the confusion of its internal conflicts, is clearly on its way toward a real proclamation, that it is facing the question of truth, that it wants more than mere blind passengers on the ship of the church. Even its liturgical formularies are being increasingly designed to engage the participation of the worshipers, to give them a place in them, to be intelligible and therefore to become a real message. But if this is so, can the church still remain an "intermediate court" for people who thus participate and have thus been challenged to come to adulthood? If this is done, can the church go on interposing itself as the real object of faith *between* them and God? The more the church becomes the place where the "Word" is proclaimed and consequently the closer it comes to the Bible, the more it can become a home in which there are only children and no slaves, in which these are only free sons and not dependents.

And even in the Orthodox Church of Russia I see this break-through to the Word taking place. I note that the functionaries of the ideological tyranny are complaining that "the cultic celebrants are putting more emphasis on the work of preaching. Today there are no services without a sermon, the purpose of which is to rouse interest in religion. The clergy are grasping every means to insure that the . . . divine meaning of the ceremonies is *explained*."[36] So the functionaries complain, and I ask myself whether in this mat-ter they do not possess the keen insight of those demons who, according to the accounts in the New Testament, have a more sensitive feeling for the presence of the Son of God than do the scribes and Pharisees. Not that the Orthodox Church is *giving up* its liturgies! It is, however, seeking to allow them to become an understandable Word which speaks to friend and foe. What before was a passing murmur that was able to touch only the numinous sensibilities now attacks the center of personality; for when any-body "speaks" he has to declare himself. He has to paint a por-trait of man and the world, a portrait of the regime and its ideology, in which those who are addressed will recognize them-selves. But because they recognize themselves, they are confronted with decision. They have to say "Yes" or cry "Ouch"! And in the article referred to, the functionaries are really roaring with pain. After the highly virulent stages of the anti-God movement they probably thought they would not have to utter another sound and could calmly contemplate this natural history museum filled with golden icons. The ongoing ceremonial, whose motor has long since been shut off, will soon quietly run down; we have lots of time!

But look what is happening; now the *Word* keeps breaking out from behind the iconostasis; now—to paraphrase Bonhoeffer—there is not only Gregorian singing, but prayers for the Jews; now the Word gets under people's skin and challenges commitment. The great silence around the altars has been broken and we are beginning to see the fulfillment of August Winnig's prediction that the time would come when the church of Russia would cease its silent celebrating and "find the Word."[37]

But we appear to be going in the *opposite* direction. We are increasingly withdrawing from the spoken word and taking refuge in ceremonies. Not that we have stopped preaching! Oh, no; the babbling goes on and the clichés keep on tumbling out—even in increased production—from the assembly line. May all those forgive me who still bear the burden of preaching the Word committed to them and are bearing faithfully and reverently; for this "holy remnant" of preachers does exist and it would be unfair to indulge in wholesale judgments. Nevertheless, the general line is flight from the Word, which is no longer ventured and therefore not found, into objective actions and the performance of sacramental acts. It may be a pious and good thing to rediscover the sacrament and the world of liturgical forms. But it is the tone that makes the music. And it is the fanfare of retreat which is being sounded here.

Therefore we ought to face the alternative, which I stated above (and in doing so broke a taboo and let out a secret of our souls), whether it would not be better to become Catholic again. Perhaps we should wait a while longer to see whether the salutary Protestant fever in the Catholic organism will come to a good conclusion and whether the new departures will bring about a new future. Perhaps on the other hand we should wait and see whether the retrograde movement in our own camp will remain irresistible. Perhaps we may have to go through a great many doctrinal discussions until we are honestly able to venture to cross the border. But the question remains. It is far more important than the yes or no answer which we may be ready to give at the moment. It is certainly not too much to say that one of the services which God demands of both sister churches is that they relentlessly question themselves and grow more mature in the process.

We have now stated the question with which the Catholic Church confronts us today. The question may be shocking. But what shocks us is probably less the question itself than the cause which prompts the question. That cause is the rubbish heap of dead words before which we stand. Even more the cause is the fact that we no longer take our own words seriously, in that we flee from them, in that we deny them their place in the center of the worship of God (and thus have already been false to the point of the Reformation!), in that we have been slipshod and allowed preaching to become contemptible prose which no editorial writer even of a mediocre daily paper would permit himself.

I do not intend to give a public or a personal answer to the question here. That would only take away from its sharpness and its relentlessness. None can be spared the torment of this *open* question. There is only one thing I can do—though without easing the torment—and that is to define the relative importance of this question. And that importance is identical with the importance which we ascribe to preaching. Here and nowhere else the decision is made concerning how we must answer the question whether we should again become Catholic.

This decision can be made only at the center of our existence. It is certainly not to be made on the basis of the question whether Protestantism can regain a position of higher standing and importance in the public eye or whether it can secure more and better broadcasting hours on radio and television, whether the meetings of the Evangelical Academies are crowded, whether losses in church membership decrease and church news receives more columns in the newspapers. All this could be nothing more than a first-class funeral. With all this we could perish lavishly. The rich man in Jesus' parable also had a "fine funeral." We ought to face the possibility that what we, in our fleshly hope, consider the "music of the future" may be only an obituary—or even the resounding thunder of a stroke of lightning which has long since found its mark.

So here the decision is not made concerning such questions as these.

It is always made at the center. It is made precisely and only on the question of what we do with the *Word* which has been committed to us.

I can understand (though not without sorrow) when someone says: "This Word is too hard for me. It demands too much of me. Let the patriarchs and prophets pray for me, let the objective treasure of ecclesiastical forms take the place of my poor feeble words. They have been tested and proved, they contain the spiritual experience of the centuries. Of course I'll go on saying my little piece in the pulpit; I'm not saying that the pulpit should disappear, leaving only the altar and lectern. But let what I say there be only a subordinate clause compared with that which is said as the principal clause in other parts of the service and which falls under the responsibility of the church. Have mercy and bear with me for trying to lessen the burden of my responsibility and allowing my preaching to be merely a parergon."

As I said, I understand such hours of discouragement and readiness to capitulate. And yet then one must also be ready to face the ultimate consequence. Then a new page of church history must be opened. Then the Reformation is finally and radically ended. Perhaps even then it was not simply a blunder, but on the whole performed a useful and productive function. But now it is really finished. It would also show more strength of character to have done with it in this way rather than to let a church go on vegetating which is only a weak, imitative second to the church of Rome.

Or—and this is the other alternative—I bestir myself from these depressing dreams and recognize the Word which has been committed to me in order that I may pass it on. I would not be the first to shrink from this task and look for a way out. And there are many such excuses: I am too young (Jer. 1:6), I am a man of unclean lips (Isa. 6:5), I am too weary, it is enough (I Kings 19:4). From the Bible alone one could gather whole batteries of arguments for keeping away from preaching. And the present time offers additional material: The word is dead even in the "managed world,"[38] it has slipped away even from the writers and poets; how then can I be an exception? Or, I am the administrator of a church plant; I have a hundred other things to do before I can prepare my sermon "in addition." Let me just hand out the accumulated treasures of faith. With them we know where we are; but as for me, I do not know where I am when the clock strikes eleven on Sundays.

As we said, the man who talks this way finds himself in good company. Even the patriarchs, prophets, and apostles indulged in this kind of disengagement.

These feelings of helplessness before the task of proclamation therefore show—and what a comfort this is!—that it is not only we today who feel that we have come to the end of the road with nothing in our hands but the ashes of an outworn and burned-out Christianity. No—even in the so-called great times of God, the times of *kairos*, there was this recoiling from proclamation. The men of God were never bold, brash pushers. For they were not like the false prophets—motivated by their will or their urge to power—but were rather fully conscious of the darkness that covers the earth and the thick darkness that weighs upon the peoples. They suffered under the incomprehensibility of God. They felt the burden of contradiction between what their hearts demanded of God and what God was actually doing, and above all what he was. Anybody who has assessed these tensions shrinks from being an instrument in that invisible hand, recoils from being sent as a light into that darkness, only to find himself a lamb among wolves. To deliver religious and philosophical addresses would not have made any difference to them. Even they perhaps might have enjoyed having their intellects titillated by discussions of the question of God. But to go out and say, "Thus says the Lord" and "Adam, where are you?" and "This is the judgment that will come upon you" and "This is the grace which is in store for you" and "In the name of the Lord, whom you do not see, I proclaim to you . . ." —this was too hard for them and here they refused to make the required leap. And I fear that if they had not felt this inhibition, they would not have understood at all what it was all about, they would not have seen that the Tremendous was casting its shadow upon them.

But not one of these men of whom the Bible speaks got past this threshold of inhibition by proceeding in the name of some categorical imperative or other and by a despairing acceptance of their duty and the obligation of their calling. On the contrary, the very message which was committed to their frightened souls also contained a promise that rescued them from fear and trembling. And that promise was that he who commanded them to speak would himself expose his Word. He would let it be *his* Word. He would allow his glory to shine through our dim and broken words. It would not be we, therefore, who would grasp his arm to liberate for him the territories over which that arm might then be outstretched. It would rather be that his arm was already stretched over the earth and we need only to walk beneath the shadow of his hand.

In Jesus' discourse in which he commissioned his disciples this is given almost incredible expression. There (Matt. 10:18 ff.) it is said that the messengers will be confronted with the great powers of this world, with authorities, public opinion, the spirit of the times, and the terror of the majority. Before these forums they will have to testify concerning one who was crucified, a man who for the serious and the snobs alike was a negligible quantity or a scandal, an insult to the intellect or a blasphemy. It is almost impossible to imagine what this confrontation means—how awkward, how painful, how humiliating it is for those who could go on living their free and easy life in all godliness and honor, what ventures of improvisation, what arduous argumentations, and what a capacity for standing firm it demands—no matter whether this means standing before a congress of philosophers concerned with the intellectual honesty of faith or the Gestapo which denies any authority beyond this world or the simple natural man who does not want to be troubled by judgment and grace. What gigantic dimensions this task takes on as soon as one thinks, not of the well-behaved sheep in the Sunday congregation and the tame citizens of the community, but of the fundamental position in which the task of preaching places a man and the elemental confrontation between the kingdom of God and the kingdom of the world which are involved in it!

Whatever is human may well begin to tremble before such a task. But what causes me to tremble also has its promise, for it says: "It is not you who stands here before governors and kings— God will acknowledge you and he will not let his Word return to him void. When it returns to you it will be freighted with the answers and the decisions of those who have heard it. And because God himself is on the battlefield, there is no need for the presumptuous assumption that the right thoughts will occur to you at the right moment. God's own Spirit will enter into you and he himself will confront men through your poor words. While you contend, Another will contend for you: "When they deliver you up, do not be anxious how you are to speak or what you are to say; for what you are to say will be given to you in that hour; for it is not you who speak, but the Spirit of your Father speaking through you."

Even promises can be frightening, and there were many moments when the men of God fled from them. The overwhelming power of what is promised, whose fulfillment I am to wait for, whose trustworthiness I am to test, on whose verification I am to stake my life—even this is oppressive. But he who is frightened in this sense is experiencing a creative terror; he is close to the core of the matter. But who has this kind of terror of preaching today?

It is not anxiety about preaching itself that gives cause for concern, but rather the *kind* of anxiety. For if all appearances are not deceiving, our anxiety is not a spiritual anxiety, not a dread of the overwhelming power of what is promised, but rather the pusillanimity of the natural homunculus, whose datebook is already filled with other engagements, the empty windbag who is afraid of being completely punctured and of betraying his futility. For the preacher betrays himself to a degree that no one else does. And he who has nothing will in the pulpit lose even what he thinks he has.

I have no desire to be so banal as simply to pump up the "courage to preach." As far as I am concerned there are some who have altogether too much courage when they let uncovered checks flutter down from the pulpit. I should rather wish that the *false* discouragement would be changed into a *right* and proper discouragement and that it would be transformed from a human sorrow into a godly sorrow. And this *godly* sorrow is present when we are frightened by the overwhelming power of the promise but nevertheless on the strength of that promise open our mouths to speak. But how can the mouth speak with authority if the heart has not first been exposed to that which here calls for an instrument and a herald?

The Misery and the Opportunity of the National Church

It has become the fashion in Germany to speak contemptuously of the national church[39] and to call it dead and outworn. The people in the church who talk in this way do not make their diagnosis more credible by the fact that they shrink from drawing the consequences which they really must draw from their diagnosis, namely, to proclaim a free church, give up church taxes, state subsidies, and legal privileges, and be content with the contributions of their congregations.

In reality the national church is not dead; it is just that people do not know what to do with it. Besides, there is no institutional structure which is in complete accord with the nature of the church. Just as we cannot be justified through works so the church cannot become pleasing to God through institutional perfection. The kingdom of God can use any form of institution as its opportunity if its people are sufficiently quick to hear, if they are obedient and resourceful enough. The devil too can use any institution as his chance if its members are deaf, indifferent, or too blindly and trustingly content with its well-oiled machinery.

This too became clear to me in America. I saw many live and vital congregations, and as far as church attendance is concerned the church there is far more a "people's church" than it is among us in Germany. Humanly speaking, the vitality of the American church is in no small measure the result of the fact that the congregations support the church by their own offerings and that therefore they are far more vitally "interested" than our more automatic tax practices would suggest. Besides, this more vital commitment is the result of the fact that the congregations are much more involved in the worship and the work of the church, that the work is carried on by numerous committees and a large proportion of the members are actively engaged by being given some kind of responsibility.

There were times during the first part of my stay in America when I thought that this was the only possible institutional solution for the church; that this is what we had to come to. So I thought until I also began to see the other side of this institutional structure and the "opportunities of the devil" inherent in it. That is to say, if a minister sets forth an opinion or a conviction of conscience which is offensive to the congregation, he may lose his position. Some rather sad examples of this can be seen in the racial struggles going on today. It must be very difficult for the pastor to preach on the Rich Young Ruler and to chide the hard-hearted rich; for the chief contributor in the congregation may be offended and transfer to another church. In addition to this is the fact that the average church member there is not much more mature than he is among us; that is to say, his criteria for judging a minister cannot exactly be called profound wisdom. Often enough he is judged by his popularity and his ability to put on attractive entertainments.

This too, of course, is an opportunity for God. For here he can test the faithfulness and steadfastness of his servants. But, as we said, it is also a chance for the devil: the temptation to be opportunistic, to compromise, and to cover up is always near.

So we should do some thinking about the institutional structures of the church. Their importance, however, should also not be overestimated, for we must remember that they are human "works" on which our salvation does not depend. To it too applies what Luther said in another connection: God knows how to carve even the rotten wood and ride the lame horse.

On the strength of this promise we must utilize the potentialities of the national church and make the most of the talent which has been entrusted to us.

To examine these potentialities fully would require another book. I content myself with two examples which illustrate what I mean.

The Search for the "Sitz im Leben"

The national church offers to children—including those from secularized homes—religious and confirmation instruction; and it also provides these children with those who are entrusted with the task of giving this instruction, namely, teachers and pastors. I am not concerned here with the particular aims and functions of religious instruction in the schools nor with the controversial problem of whether it should be confessional instruction in the faith or simply objective information. I am rather concerned with a completely different side of the matter. And it is my observation that rather strangely only a few have seen this side of the matter.

Because the national church thus has contact with children who come from various backgrounds of religion and attitudes toward life, it also has access to their parents. Parents will always be interested in those who are interested in their children.

This could look like a tactical recommendation, an opportunistic search for ways of gaining access. It could, for example, be misunderstood in a sentimental sense that the pastor could creep into the good graces of parents by being "so very nice to our little one," or that he could melt even secularized hearts by this sentimental dodge. Now it would be dishonest to deny that very earnest and sincere pastoral procedures can be linked with tactical considerations. But then how foolish it would be to speak of this as being *merely* tactics! If that were the case, we would also have to interpret Jesus' saying, "Seek ye first the kingdom of God and all these things shall be added unto you," as being merely a tactical counsel. In other words, the best tactical procedure for anybody who wants all these other things (prestige, human affection, and material blessings) would be to seek first the kingdom of God. Or the best method of insuring that your "days may be long in the land" is to adopt the tactic of "honoring your father and mother." How absurd it is to speak of tactics here! But this business of being overcome by what is actually an old-maidish fear even of raising tactical considerations seems to be a perverted by-product of the Reformation doctrine that it is the Word of God that does everything by itself without the co-operation of man. A quite different conclusion would be in accord with the Reformation way of thinking: not to despise good works—and therefore tactical approaches—but rather to assign to them a relative, auxiliary importance and thus not to allow them to be the *determinative* thing.

Consequently, it is not a question of eliminating works and tactics, but rather of giving them their proper place within the Christian life.

The significance of this practical, subordinate, subservient character of the tactical can readily be seen in connection with our problem of the national church. I said that through the children the church also has access to the parents. I would describe the practical significance of this access as follows. Every educational task confronts persons with "ultimate" questions. It makes us realize that the little person is something given which cannot simply be formed and molded as we may wish but must be accepted. It confronts us with responsibility for another living person who is entrusted to us and is not merely there for the enrichment of our own existence. It confronts us with the mystery of evil and hence with everything that is related to forgiving and pardoning. It confronts us with the task of loving, the claims of which can never be met by a natural love, but must also come to terms with what is unlovable and questionable in the other person. And finally it is constantly leading us beyond the material problems of food, clothing, and shelter to the horizon of human existence as a whole: its purpose, its goal, its meaning. To what and for what am I to educate, what picture is to be developed upon this sensitive plate? These are questions which really touch the ultimate.

And these are exactly the questions with which faith, and therefore pastoral care too, has to do. They are coded forms of the question of the creation, the justification, and the destination of man. When as pastors we talk to parents about their children and deal with the problem of educational responsibility—including such concrete things as a child's lying and a teenager's choice of vocation—we can hardly do anything else but bring out these ultimate aspects of life. We bring the gospel into play in so far as it contains affirmations concerning the questions which are already existent and relevant in the educational situation and which we therefore do not need first to bring out. We allow the gospel to be heard as another reading of the questions of life, and on these questions other people and other authorities—"common sense," the parents themselves, who naturally have some ideas about these problems, teachers, philosophers, editorial writers, neighbors, maiden aunts, and many others—also have something to say. The gospel emerges in competition with many other diagnosticians and therapists—just as the church in a pluralistic society likewise emerges as one voice among many others. Here the gospel offers itself to be tried and proved as a solution. Here it is offered as an answer to the question which is raised. Hence there is no need to cast about for points of contact or to elicit artificially the proper questions.

The observation of this situation leads to some extremely important meditations upon the history of thought and theology. In rather roughly abbreviated form, the change that has taken place may be expressed as follows.

Originally theological work was carried on by dealing with the dogmas in the narrower sense of the word. The first Christian centuries were filled with controversy over the doctrinal comprehension of the person of Christ and the Trinity. But very early, and then more clearly in the age of the Reformation, and then very systematically since the Enlightenment, men began to ask what *"Sitz im Leben"* these dogmas had, what relevance they had to our life situation. The greatness of theologians like Lessing[40] and Schleiermacher lies in the fact that they were concerned about this *"Sitz im Leben."* They started from the recognition that I can appropriate and receive into my existence only that which ultimately concerns me and therefore has meaning for my life. Since that time it has been the task of theology to demonstrate the "existential relevance" of the dogmas and doctrines of the church. In line with what we said concerning preaching, we can also characterize the trends of modern theology by saying that its aim has been to show that "I am in the picture," that it "concerns me." I can believe only if this is clear to me. In other words, I must see that the "one thing needful" is really necessary. If I do not see this, then, as far as I am concerned, the most elementary access to faith is blocked. Then I can be only a "dependent" or one who passively goes along without any real, personal commitment, subjecting myself to the law of inertia in tradition.

I am now of the conviction that we are entering a new phase in the history of thought, and to me it seems very important that we should clearly recognize this transition. Today the "Christian engagement" is again beginning at a *different* point. Our question— in any case the question of the secularized man, in so far as he is receptive and asks the question at all—no longer begins with the given dogmas and asks what is their "*Sitz im Leben.*" For many the dogmas are no longer "given" at all, but are completely unreal. Our situation is rather that we are oppressed by very definite problems whose "*Sitz im Leben*" is quite obvious.

Among these problems there is, for example, the question of our finitude. Today, it seems to me, we are living in constant meditation upon death, though nobody will say a word about dying. (Existential philosophy, however, is always talking about it!) We know that youth passes away, that we must taste and savor everything while we can, because what is past will never come again. We go rushing on, trying to get through everything we want from life, for we know that time is irreversible. We protest against age and idolize youth. And many seek to preserve the mask of youth or daub it on artificially. Temporality and finitude are problems whose "*Sitz im Leben*" is unmistakable and undisputed.

All faculties and professions have such problems which are rooted in life. Medicine asks what really constitutes health and why human life is inviolable. The jurists ask, in view of the threatening positivism of law, where the ultimate normative authority is to be found—in natural law, in the commandments of God, in common sense? The technologists ask (or men ask in view of technology) whether it is not leading to a world of "perfect means and confused ends" (as Albert Einstein once expressed it). So education too confronts us with questions of elemental and existential import.

When we bring the gospel into contact with these given questions, the question where it has its "Sitz im Leben" becomes anachronistic; for we are starting from this life situation! We are already *there*, and we have *discovered* that we are there.

The order of the question therefore runs in reverse direction from the way it ran formerly. We no longer start with the dogmas and ask what is their "Sitz im Leben"; rather we come from the "Sitz im Leben" and there let the gospel become a question or an answer or another reading or *other* answers which have already been given.

Naturally, this has been stated in a much simplified way. We must not think of this reversal of the process as being so simple that these questions which have their root in life are already prepared for us, already cut out so that they fit precisely into the gears of the gospel. The questions which confront us in the educational situation have already shown us that this is *not* so. The fact that my child is "given" does not by any means automatically elicit the question of creation. The fact that I discover evil in him does not spontaneously generate the question of the nature of sin. And the task of having to excuse him does not as a matter of course point to forgiveness and justification. It is true that some rather shallow-minded apologists have always thought this way, but it is not so. The problems which have their "Sitz im Leben" are often like the proverbial bells: we hear them all right, but we do not know what they are saying. We doubtless hear these elementary questions, we may even be oppressed by them, but in the last analysis we do not know *what* it is they are asking. This hidden thrust of the question must first be elicited.

The way this occurs can be observed in Jesus' dialogues with people. He always lays hold of the question with which people have approached him. But he never answers it directly, or more precisely, he never regards the question as a finished form into which the answer of his message will fit without further ado. Rather he first corrects the way the question is put, he brings out its hidden thrust, which the questioners were not yet aware of at all. Most of them did not realize *what* they were asking and *what* was oppressing them.

A New Style of Proclamation: Parents Groups

So it is when the gospel encounters the problems of education: it does not simply answer the questions, but first formulates and restates the questions which are already present in raw form in the life situation.

This confronts us with a new task and also a new style of Christian proclamation. Here we stand at the beginning of a new Christian era. When we founded the Evangelical Academies in 1945 we had at least a vague feeling that we were crossing this threshold. We were searching for a new form of proclamation which would meet the needs of that time of collapse after the war. We believed that people brought with them their elementary questions. The ideological dominion had collapsed and quite literally the bottom had dropped out of life. People were seeking norms and standards, they were looking for meaning and, against the background of an era of contempt for man, they were asking what was the value of human life. And here, we thought, the gospel should be on the scene to bring out the hidden thrust of these questions, to solve or to relieve people of the torment of these questions. The Evangelical Academies—which were soon joined by similar movements in the Catholic Church—were the institutional expression of this new task and this new form of proclamation. It is manifest that this task and this form of proclamation must not be allowed to remain limited to this institutional expression but that it must also find its place in the parishes and congregations and that there are many possible variations of it.

We are confronted with one of these possible variations when we take another look at the problems of education. Once they are recognized as questions which have their *"Sitz im Leben,"* it is precisely the national church situation which presents some definite tasks of providing a special kind of proclamation and also appropriate institutional solutions. One such solution would be the establishment of parents groups within the local congregations. Through the situation of parenthood we would have in these groups what Paul Tillich calls the correlation "of the questions implied in the situation with the answers implied in the message."[41] And as the church speaks to questions which have their *"Sitz im Leben,"* then it will also be seen that this Word of the church has this elemental character or at least the opportunity will be offered to see that this is so.

And still another thing would be achieved. The church would thus gather together a group of people who are really living in the midst of life, who are therefore what we called "historical people." In another connection we spoke of the vicious circle to which preaching is so largely subjected, namely, that its Docetic character attracts only "historyless" (mostly old) people and that then the gathering of older and largely middle-class people intensifies still further the Docetic tendency of preaching. This vicious circle could be broken with the help of parents groups. In these groups it is quite impossible to speak Docetically, unless one is prepared to see them immediately take flight again. Here one is compelled to deal with the detail, the practical, concrete issues of life, and the Word must become flesh. And if one fails here, then this is a judgment on the preaching itself. But if some new breakthroughs are made here, the stimulus will have its effect upon the preaching that is done in the pulpit and it will immunize it against Docetism. If I had been compelled to accept the office of bishop, I would have concentrated all our energies upon this point to break out of our paralysis. At this point the national church would be seen to be not a mere mortgage but rather as an opportunity and a promise.

Confirmation—the Thorny Question

At the present time the weakest point in the national church is the practice of confirmation. Note that I say not "confirmation" but the "practice" of confirmation. With all the perspicacity of the demons the Communist regime in East Germany has spotted this weakest point and set up its own "youth dedication" (*Jugendweihe*), a fairly successful competitor of the church's confirmation. But in Western Germany too there is a great deal of uneasiness about it. We are deeply disturbed by the fact that there is so much uncertainty and unclarity about it, indeed, that it may even be full of lies. The family celebrations after confirmation are usually occasions for a great party which often ends in general befuddlement. The poor victims no longer receive a copy of Gerok's *Palm Branches*, bound in leather with gold edges, which they never read; but they do receive tape recorders, neckties, dress clothes, and Beatle records. The churches are full of people who act like a foreign occupation army on church territory. They seem not to have the faintest idea of the country and its customs. And the one thing that distinguishes them from military invaders is that they are much more timid and helpless in their behavior. (Might not parents groups help to remedy this misery?)

But it is perhaps the ministers who suffer most because of this situation, since they know what it is all about and what for most of the participants it is *not* all about. They know the tremendous responsibility that is laid upon them and do not know how to meet it. In their honesty they tremble at the institutional lie which it represents. Many of them suffer to the point of heartsickness. They suffer over what has been committed to them. No wonder that here the church has become involved in experimentation and is seeking for some way out. I do not pretend to know a way out. But I have given some thought to some angles which may perhaps be helpful in finding a way out.

Confirmation arose as a kind of practical supplementation of the practice of *infant baptism*. We need not discuss here the fact that infant baptism itself has again become a problem nor the extent to which it is being challenged. If it is to be justified theologically, this can be done only by emphasizing that it expresses the prevenient character of divine grace and by teaching that parents and sponsors are to be understood as the church which accepts responsibility for the child and its nurture in faith. And here again I forbear to point out what has become of our office of sponsorship and how the degeneration of this office threatens to reduce infant baptism to a bizarre caricature.

In any case, if in baptism the child is transferred to the responsibility of the church and its representatives (parents and sponors), then this responsibility cannot be thought of as being exclusive, but only as inclusive. That is to say, the church assumes the responsibility not simply vicariously and therefore "in the stead" of the baptized child, but rather assumes the obligation to lead the child to grow into its own, adult acceptance of responsibility. The aim can only be the confirmand's mature and voluntary acceptance of his baptism as an infant, his ratification, so to speak, of the baptismal covenant or "contract." To this extent it corresponds to infant baptism. Both together constitute an indivisible whole.

Naturally, this ratification can be given only if the confirmand is making an adult decision. And here is where the difficulty comes in. This is where the dishonesty lurks. That is to say, since it has been recognized that such a ratification of the baptismal vow by a fourteen-year-old would be a lie, the conclusion has not been drawn (as it has in some other countries) that we must therefore postpone confirmation to the age of sixteen or eighteen. We have rather said: We cannot honestly demand a binding confession, and when we do this, we make of confirmation a mere observance of the conclusion of instruction and interpret the confirmand's confession as meaning not much more than an acknowledgment of having "taken due note of the doctrines."

This, it is true, leaves one in a state of commendable honesty, but it also means that one has quite radically given up the meaning of confirmation as being the ratification of the baptismal vow. But it also means that one has thereby stripped infant baptism of its meaning and reduced it to a mere ecclesiastical custom, in other words, to a farce.

Having said this so harshly, I feel the need to add that I do not wish it to sound pharisaical. For I speak as an outsider who had to endure the hardness of this situation only for a relatively short time. Therefore it is very easy for me to criticize. And I have a profound sympathy for my brethren in the practical ministry who have been pitched into this muddle which has gradually come into being over the years. I know their suffering and I know how they are struggling to find a solution. And I can judge what it must mean for them to have to go on with this old routine until some liberating way out is found.

Nevertheless, even if we so denature confirmation that it is nothing more than an acknowledgment of having taken due note of certain doctrines, there is still the question of the proper age for confirmation. And even on this (dubious!) level, the age of fourteen seems to be questionable. There are two reasons which have been given for questioning the age of fourteen, one of which seems to me to be serious and the other stupid.

The serious reason consists in the argument that the age of puberty with its confusions and adolescent interests does not seem to be the time of life which is particularly suited for a concentration upon the essentials and the clarification of the far-reaching questions of life. If I am not mistaken, Adolf von Harnack went so far as to make the bold proposal that religious instruction be suspended altogether during this critical period. In any case it is certainly not immediately obvious that confirmation should be located specifically in this period of life.

The stupid reason (at any rate it seems to *me* to be stupid) consists in the concern that confirmation may be drawn into the updraft of the time when youngsters finish school and enter into life. This, it is argued, makes confirmation a kind of sacred glorification of an important turning point in life and thus threatens to make it only a means to an end.

This scruple seems to me to be foolish for two reasons. First, because it certainly makes good sense to see such a turning point in life *sub specie aeternitatis* and also to understand confirmation —along with its relationship to baptism!—as an interpretation of the way from birth to now and the way "to the open sea" of life. Actually what we have here is the classical instance of the situation where a problem which has its *"Sitz im Leben"* is crying out for an answer and opportunity is given to see that the message is elementally related to life. Out of sheer anxiety that they will be accused of being opportunistic some people seem to be ready to break off any relationship of the gospel to concrete life situations —and thus perhaps unconsciously give further impetus to the trend toward Docetism.

Second, because the same argument could be used to reject infant baptism, sick communion, church marriage, and funerals. Here too it is quite possible that the situation may be the real motive and that the act of the church may be given the role of providing a sacral glorification to the occasion, thus making it a dubious means to an end. There is no doubt that this danger, this yearning for ritual and ceremony on the part of average people, does exist. But here again we must remember that danger is not a theological term and that alongside of the possiblility of miscarriage it also contains challenges and opportunities, for, after all, now the pastor can *say* something other than what people *expect* him to say!

But if—for serious or stupid reasons—it is not desirable to confirm at the age of fourteen, then in any case it is completely absurd to lower the age and confirm at twelve or younger. This way out, which addresses itself to youngsters who are intellectually and spiritually defenseless, seems to be more than dubiously subject to the law of least resistance.

This applies not only to confirmation itself but above all to the preceding instruction which concludes with confirmation at this time. At this age the Bible stories can be told only in the simplest fashion and the catechisms can only be memorized. At this age we cannot even begin to address ourselves to problems which the "enlightened" person will later have to grapple with if he is to bring the Christian message into relation with his "modern knowledge"—his for the most part half-educated knowledge!—and his particular life problems. The consequence of breaking off instruction at such an early age will then be that the "Christian religion" will more than ever live on in the adult mind as something that belongs to the fairyland of childhood and is revived in memory by all the sentimentality of Christmas.

This proposal to move confirmation to an earlier age is therefore equivalent to a capitulation. It appears to be determined by the resigned attitude which says: Well, we won't get them later anyhow. But will not those whom we "get" at this age drift away from us later in an even more helpless condition? Will they not say: Childhood, where all this religion belongs, is now over?

In all probability the change that is taking place in the school situation will help us in our search for new ways of solving the problem (in any case if we get away from the misgivings about having confirmation coincide with the time when a youngster finishes school). For sooner or later the time of school-leaving will be lengthened by one or two years, bringing the pupils closer to what in the higher schools is called a middle stage of maturation. This would bring us into the time of beginning adulthood and then—on the basis of the youngsters' greater freedom to make their own decisions and therefore not on the basis of a general collective—we could expect them to carry out the ratification of infant baptism of which we spoke. What is needed is broad, high-level preparation for the changes that are coming. This means plans of instruction and organizational forms, and I can only hope that there are committees which have already begun to work on these plans.

Concerning the details of the task nothing more can be said here, except that they must meet the requirement of being flexible and adaptable to the age groups concerned. Therefore of the plans that I know the one that appeals to me most is a graded two-stage plan. The first stage would cover an instruction period of six months to a year to prepare for reception into the communing congregation and thus into full membership in the Body of Christ. The second stage of at least a year's instruction would lead up to the time of school-leaving and end with the actual confirmation. This would be followed by a third stage of voluntary instruction.

This particular plan, however, is suggested only as an example, a possibility that is worth considering. More important than a concrete solution at this time, however, is that the church administrations not only grant the freedom to pursue experimental solutions but actually encourage and support them. In the educational field we know the advantages of establishing model schools. We ought to create similar opportunities for confirmation instruction and confirmation itself. We are suffering from the increasing bureaucratization and centralization of the church. We get an almost apocalyptic picture when we visualize plans being hatched out for the renewal of confirmation possibly by the same kind of official boards and committees which have provided us with re-pristinated liturgies and being flooded by a golden shower of "ancient treasures." In such a thorny and ticklish matter, which would have to be guided with the utmost caution, it would really be dreadful to be provided with directives "from above" and to find the new reality all laid out beforehand in ecclesiastical laws, rubrics, and regulations. Here is where a revolution "from below" would do us good. Here is where experimentation on the part of courageous and resourceful congregations as well as of imaginative pastors is needed. During this transitional period the church administrations should function essentially only in an advisory, co-ordinating capacity, serving in the exchange of experience and setting generous limits to the experimentation. This would be an example of liturgy in the institutional realm, in that here the congregations would not be regarded merely as objects and audiences but rather given a vital sense of self-responsibility and even challenged to use their imagination.

Suffering Love for the Church

In concluding this self-criticism of the church the author addresses a critical question to himself. The fact is that this question has troubled him from the first moment, indeed, long before he began to write this book. The question is this: Dare anyone who suffers because of "the trouble with the church" write about it publicly? Ought he not to hide from the eyes of strangers what makes him suffer and feel miserable as an object of shame?

Now, if he were an atheist, there could be no question of his being permitted to speak openly. Then the very existence of the church as such would be an offense to him and its empirical form would be a further offense. To him it would be a symbol of power-hungry clericalism, obscurantism, confessional strategy, and enslavement of conscience. For him it would actually be a point of honor to trumpet abroad his criticism and bell this sneaky cat.

But when one's suffering because of the church comes not from indignation but from a suffering love for it—dare one *then* confess this suffering openly? Dare one thus give to those of ill will the chance to equate the complaint of love and the pain of commitment with the criticism of those who stand aloof and outside the church, which they utter in anger or superiority, cynically or patronizingly, but always without being touched or committed in any way? Was not Heinrich Böll's criticism of *his* church (the Catholic Church) misinterpreted in exactly the same way? Was it not interpreted almost as a public renunciation, though it was clearly marked by the anger and pain of a lover? Should one not rather whisper about it in secret and only to intimates instead of shouting it from the housetops?

As the preceding chapters show, the author has decided to speak openly and to overcome his fear of being misunderstood. I see the number of those who are leaving the church—not outwardly perhaps and not officially—progressively increasing. I see some quiet unconscious developments taking place whose explosive power is hardly less than that which is sought for in the consciously planned strategy of the ideological tyrannies.

In the context of this theme I see two other factors. First, I believe that I can see that the sad, angry, or indifferent attitude of resignation on the part of those who take their leave in disinterest rests upon the same offenses that trouble me. If I were not bound with every fiber of my being to what the church believes—oh, why should I speak in such a furtive way?—if I were not convinced that Christ is risen and that he lives, I would probably have spoken the same way they have,[42] and I probably could not have drawn any other conclusion except that of leaving the church. For apart from this one thing that will not let me go, the church in its empirical form would have little attraction for me. Only the friends I have in it, those who bravely endure and persevere in a life of devotion and sacrifice, would make it hard for me to leave. And what binds me to them most of all is precisely this, that they suffer because of the church just as I do.

But if it is true that people are leaving the church or remaining indifferent to it for the same reasons which cause me to suffer because of the church—except that the "deserters" see these painful things from the outside, while I see them as a participant and a lover from the inside—then must I not speak about it openly? Must I not show these disillusioned and sometimes despairing people who have become disaffected from the church that what appears to them to be dead and outworn is perhaps actually a corpse—not only rendered obsolete and thrown on the scrap heap by *history*, as they imagine, but actually murdered by lovelessness and idolatry in its own ranks? Must I not show them that it is the poor mutilated body of the Lord, whose Head is still living, however, and therefore still has the promise of new life? The valley of dry bones is waiting for the awakening Spirit. And to whom is this Spirit promised if not to those who have begun to discover the monstrousness of this field of dead bones and trust the God of life?

Would not then the one legitimate form in which one may preach and missionize today be to speak in this way of *suffering* because of the church? Is it not possible that this kind of honest proclamation would make people stop and listen, if such a confession made it clear that suffering from the church does not kill our love for it (as one might expect) but rather deepens it? Could not such a confession prompt people to ask *what* it is that is still worth loving in it and that more than outweighs our suffering and trouble with it?

And I see a second factor and that is that the question of what the church should proclaim has by no means ceased to be asked, but rather that our generation—especially the young people—is full of "hunger and thirst for righteousness." Wherever there is vital preaching (no matter whether it be Catholic or Protestant, in summer camps or at home) people still come flocking to hear it, and again, especially the young people. In innumerable discussions the question of religion makes itself felt, either in disguised or overt form. And still today, as was always the case, wherever anyone comes as a Christian or a Christian minister or theologian people will speak to him about questions of faith and he enjoys a confidence and esteem in all questions of human trust which actually puts him to shame, unless he is a strange kind of a saint or the Docetic type we have described. The fields are ripe for the harvest. But the laborers are few—and few also are the shepherds who do not merely linger in the enclosed pastures but go out to seek those who have strayed.

This little book is meant to be a conversation, carried on in the light of the promise, between those who mourn and suffer because of the trouble with the church. "Blessed are those who mourn, for they shall be comforted." That blessing applies here too.

In Conclusion[43]

Spiritual processes cannot be described without emphasis upon the *place* where they can occur. The man who does not work at the art of preaching without ulterior purpose, but who is always thinking of how the article will sell and perhaps also of how he can keep the market going, becomes a *routinier*; he becomes a servant, not of the kingdom of God, but of the task of perfecting the preaching machinery. What he says may be "legitimate"; and the way he puts it may be a masterpiece of ecclesiastical "strategy." And yet what comes out will be a paradoxical self-refutation of the message, because his own existence testifies against it. What then takes place—all very correctly and in accord with the rules of the art—is the mere threshing of empty straw. The well-oiled machine no longer serves; it makes propaganda for an institution which, after all, should itself be only a servant. What the church then does is simply an act of self-assertion on the part of one institution engaged in competition with other institutions.

The result of all this may be some kind of success, but it is not the fruit of the Spirit. It may be quite possible to register certain influences that the church has exerted upon public life, but they are not the salt that preserves from decay nor the leaven that determines the taste of the bread. The grain of wheat of the messenger and the grain of wheat of the church as institution must first be hidden in the earth, in quietness and calm passivity; it must first die if it is to be able to spring up and bear fruit. Yet we work feverishly, pushing things along with artificial fertilizers; we are perpetual "producers," worshiping the gods of production. That is why the valley of dry bones spreads all around us. We are pragmatists, awed by the art of influencing people; we have forgotten the lesson of the grain of wheat about dying in order to be. Only he who dies and rises again with Christ can credibly bear witness to the death and resurrection of the Lord. But because we do not live in the magnetic field of Good Friday and Easter we merely act "as if" he had risen again. That is why the handy formulas and well-aimed addresses help us not a bit. The enemy who goes about at night, sowing his weeds among the grains of wheat which we have ostensibly scattered in the name of Jesus Christ, is the Grand Inquisitor who comes from our own midst and organizes the Christian enterprise with a view to success. He who has ears to hear, let him hear!

Notes

1. *Poesie und Leben* in *Gesammelte Werke; Prosa*, Bd. I, p. 265.
2. In my *Theologische Ethik* (Theological Ethics), I, Third Edition (1956), I have tried to set forth the misunderstandings of the doctrine of the two kingdoms that a person must have fallen into in order to succumb to such extreme errors.
3. Martin Kähler, *Theologe und Christ* (1926), p. 113.
4. Cf. my book, *Encounter with Spurgeon* (Philadelphia: Fortress Press, 1963).
5. Cf. n. 4.
6. E.g. I Cor. 14. Cf. the chapter on glossolalia in my book *Between Heaven and Earth, Conversations with American Christians* (New York: Harper & Row, 1965), pp. 88 ff.
7. *Gesammelte Werke; Prosa*, Bd. II 1951, pp. 7-20 (Ausg., H. Steiner).
8. On the extensive literature concerning this fictitious letter cf. especially the excellent study by H. J. Mähl, *"Die Mystik der Worte. zum Sprachproblem i.d. modernen dt. Dichtung"* in *Wirkendes Wort, Jahrg.* 13, 5, pp. 289 ff.
9. *Gesammelte Werke; Prosa*, Bd. I, pp. 264 f.
10. *Schriften*, II, p. 378.
11. *Gesammelte Werke*, ed. Wellershoff, I, pp. 528 f.
12. Quoted in Margarete Susman, *Ich habe viele Leben gelebt* (Stuttgart, 1964), pp. 22 f.
13. Friedrich Hauss, *Der Heilsweg. Predigten von D. Aloys Henhöfer* (Karlsruhe: n.d.), p. 4.
14. Rev. 12:12.
15. Ps. 31:15.

16. Cf. Hermann Diem. *Warum Textpredigt?* (München, 1939).
17. Quoted in O. H. Frommel, *Frommels Lebensbild,* II (Berlin: 1901), p. 305.
18. Here I take up some ideas which I have already dealt with in my book *Between Heaven and Earth, Conversations with American Christians* (New York: Harper & Row, 1965). I am so much concerned with these thoughts, however, that I must refer to them again in this connection.
19. *Word and Faith* (Philadelphia: Fortress Press, 1963), p. 198.
20. *Glaube und Verstehen,* II (1952), pp. 59 ff., especially p. 68. Translation taken from Rudolf Bultmann, *Essays Philosophical and Theological,* tr. by James C. G. Greig (New York: The Macmillan Company, 1955), pp. 77 f.
21. Cf. my *Theologische Ethik,* I, § 2144 ff., and *Geschichte und Existenz,* 2. Aufl. (Gütersloh: 1964), pp. 66 ff.
22. O. F. Bollnow, "Existenzphilosophie," in *Systematische Philosophie,* ed. Nikolai Hartmann (Stuttgart-Berlin: 1942), p. 349.
23. *Ibid.,* p. 356.
24. I have dealt with this in my *Ethics of Sex* (New York: Harper & Row, 1964), pp. 26 ff.
25. In what follows I draw from the foreword to the second edition of my book *Geschichte und Existenz* (Gütersloh: 1964).
26. Luke 10:29.
27. Matt. 5:28.
28. Matt. 5:38 ff.
29. Those who have theological background know how Luther expressed this contradiction in the terms *opus proprium* (proper work) and *opus alienum* (strange work). I have attempted to set forth the problems which this presents as being actually the central questions of theological anthropology and cosmology (*Theologische Ethik,* I and II, 1). Cf. also my *Geschichte und Existenz* (1964)—Ordnungslehre.
30. I cannot deal further with the problem and its solution here. I have done this at length in my *Theologische Ethik,* especially in the section on the autonomisms in the *Ethik des Politischen,* II, 2.
31. Wolfgang Trillhaas, a preacher and professor (Göttingen), has also published a work on ethics: *Ethik* (Berlin, 1959). (Trans.)
32. Quoted by Eberhard Bethge, "*Dietrich Bonhoeffer. Person und Werk,*" *Die Mündige Welt* (Munich: Chr. Kaiser Verlag, 1955), p. 23. (Trans.)

33. The author has expressed convictions similar to those in this section in previous publications; cf. *Voyage to the Far East* (Philadelphia: Fortress Press, 1962), pp. 173 ff., 177 ff., 188 ff., *The Freedom of the Christian Man* (New York: Harper & Row, 1963), pp. 182 ff. (Trans.)
34. Mark 5:25 ff.
35. *Widerstand und Ergebung,* p. 193; see ET, *Prisoner for God,* p. 131. Translation mine. (Trans.)
36. Cf. with this and what follows the Communist interpretation of this break-through to proclamation in *Partijnaja,* No. 22, 1958, German translation in *Ostprobleme,* 1959, 1, pp. 25 ff., especially p. 27.
37. *Europa. Gedanken eines Deutschen* (1937) p. 43.
38. Cf. K. Korn, *Sprache in der verwalteten Welt* (1962).
39. *Volkskirche,* literally folk church, people's church, established church, or national church. (Trans.)
40. On this cf. my book *Offenbarung, Vernunft und Existenz, Studien zur Religionsphilosophie Lessings,* 4. Aufl. (Gütersloh, 1959).
41. *Systematic Theology* (Chicago: University of Chicago Press, 1951), I, p. 8. (Trans.)
42. Cf. Ps. 73:15.
43. I borrow the following section from the introduction to my book *Encounter with Spurgeon* (Philadelphia: Fortress Press, 1963), pp. 13 f.

Sources of the Epigraphs

Margarete Susmann. *Ich habe viele Leben gelebt,* 1964.
Hans Domizlaff, *Denkfehler. Imaginäre Vortrage,* 1964.
Ernst Jünger, *An der Zeitmauer,* 1959.
Martin Kähler, *Geschichte der protestantische Dogmatik im* 19. *Jahrhundert.* Hrsg. von Ernst Kähler, 1962.
Martin Kähler, *Theologe und Christ,* 1926.
Georges Bernanos, *The Diary of a Country Priest,* tr. by Pamela Morris (New York: The Macmillan Company, 1937), p. 122.

Index

Aeschylus, 27
Agamemnon, 35
Agape, 70
Anthropology, 67, 69, 76
Augustine, 51

Baptism, infant, 121, 123
Barth, Karl, 62, 64
Benn, Gottfried, 45, 46
Bible, see Holy Scriptures
Böll, Heinrich, 127
Bonhoeffer, Dietrich, 13, 33, 84, 94, 99, 104
Brecht, Bert, 5, 46, 47
Broch, Hermann, 46
Bultmann, Rudolf, 67, 69

Calvin, John, 1, 59, 60
Catholicism, 84, 89, 91, 97, 102 ff., 127
Christology, 66 f.
Confessing Church, 12
Confirmation, 120 ff.
Credibility, the preacher's, 3 ff. 15, 16, 18, 51, 130
Cyrus, 7

Death, 21, 22, 116
Demosthenes, 43

Docetism, 66 ff., 71, 74, 76, 77, 78, 79, 80, 85, 119, 123, 128

Ebeling, Gerhard, 67
Einstein, Albert, 117
Eros, 70
Eschatology, 55, 56, 76
Evangelical Academies, 77, 105, 118
Existentialism, 69, 116

Faith, 34, 53, 54, 94, 114
Forgiveness, 114, 117

German Faith Movement, 37
Glossolalia, 33
Good Samaritan, parables of, 13 f., 73
Gospel, 32, 55, 78, 79, 114 f., 117
Grace, 2, 7, 8, 10, 11, 36, 38, 47, 108, 121
Guardino, Romano, 91

Harnack, Adolf, 35, 122
Heidegger, Martin, 35, 69
Hemingway, Ernest, 46
Henhöfer, Aloys, 55
Heresy, 40
Hofmannsthal, Hugo von, 3, 44 f.
Holy Scriptures, 9, 53, 54, 59 f., 62, 65, 90, 99, 103, 107, 108

Homer, 27
Hypocrisy, 3, 5, 10, 14

Irenaeus, 51

Jaspers, 69, 73
Jews, the, 13, 20 f., 39, 54, 85, 104
Judgment, 7, 57, 68, 108
Justification, 2, 48 56, 61, 90, 94, 95, 96, 111, 114, 117

Kafka, Franz, 5, 39
Kähler, Martin, 14, 39
Kant, Immanuel, 74
Kierkegaard, Søren, 14, 47, 77

Language and preaching, 35 ff., 42 ff.
Leppich, Pater, 91
Lessing, G. E., 115
"Liturgism," 49, 83 ff., 92, 94 ff.
Liturgy, 10, 38, 84, 100 ff.
Logos, 33 f.
Logos spermaticos, 33 f.
Lord's Prayer, the, 54, 75
Love, 23, 70 ff., 91, 114
Luther, 1, 12, 15, 17, 51, 53, 59, 60, 61, 66, 77, 95, 98, 112
Lutheranism, 12, 85, 92

Machiavelli, Niccolò, 71
Mao Tse-tung, 4
Meaning of life, 21, 23, 65
Meaninglessness, 8, 53
Menelaus, 35
Menken, Gottfried, 63
Musil, Robert, 39

National Socialism, 12
Nebuchadnezzar, 7
Nolde, Emil, 5
Novalis, 45

Paul, 27, 33, 37
Plato, 34, 35

Prayer, 25
Priesthood of believers, 30
Protestantism, 12, 15, 90, 102

Rahner, Karl, 81
Rationalism, 36, 85, 99
Reformation, the, 1, 28, 48, 86, 90, 94, 95, 102 ff., 115
Reformers, the, 30
Resurrection, 35, 55
Russian Orthodox Church, 103 f.

Sartre, Jean-Paul, 69
Schlatter, Adolf, 27
Schleiermacher, Friedrich, 28, 51, 115
Schweitzer, Albert, 18
Self-love, 71
Sermon on the Mount, 74 f., 96
Sex, 11, 35
Sin, 2, 8, 36, 38, 47, 75, 117
Spinoza, 28
Spirit, Holy, 8, 10, 25, 48, 49, 51, 54, 97, 109, 128, 129
Spurgeon, Charles Haddon, 31
Stoic philosophy, 34, 35

Theology and preaching, 25 ff., 56 ff., 65 ff.
Thompson, Francis, 67, 68, 69
Tillich, Paul, 119
Tradition, 4, 97
Trillhaas, Wolfgang, 78
Two kingdoms, doctrine of, 12

Williams, Tennessee, 5
Winnig, August, 104
Witness, 16, 42, 50, 51, 56, 130
Word of God, 40, 48, 84, 98, 103, 104, 106, 108, 109, 113, 119

Xenophon, 27

Zahrnt, Heinz, 26

Format by Cynthia Muser
Set in Linotype Electra
Composed, printed and bound by The Haddon Craftsmen, Inc.
HARPER & ROW, PUBLISHERS, INCORPORATED